The Corgi Series

GLYN JONES

The Corgi Series *Writing from Wales*

1 Dannie Abse, *Touch Wood*
2 Idris Davies, *A Carol for the Coalfield*
3 Mike Jenkins, *Laughter Tangled in Thorn*
4 *War*, an anthology edited by Dewi Roberts
5 Alun Richards, *Scandalous Thoughts*
6 Alun Lewis, *The Sentry*
7 Tony Curtis, *Considering Cassandra*
8 *Love*, an anthology edited by Dewi Roberts
9 Raymond Garlick, *The Delphic Voyage*
10 Rhys Davies, *Nightgown*
11 Sheenagh Pugh, *What If This Road*
12 *Places*, an anthology edited by Dewi Roberts
13 Leslie Norris, *Water*
14 T. H. Jones, *Lucky Jonah*
15 Paul Henry, *The Breath of Sleeping Boys*
16 *Work*, an anthology edited by Dewi Roberts
17 Harri Webb, *The Stone Face*
18 Geraint Goodwin, *The Shearing*
19 John Ormond, *Boundaries*
20 *Landscapes*, an anthology edited by Dewi Roberts
21 Glyn Jones, *The Common Path*
22 Gwyn Thomas, *Land! Land!*
23 Emyr Humphreys, *The Rigours of Inspection*
24 *Death*, an anthology edited by Dewi Roberts

The Corgi Series *Writing from Wales*

Glyn Jones

The Common Path
poems and a story

Series editor
Meic Stephens
Emeritus Professor of Welsh Writing in English
University of Glamorgan

Carreg Gwalch Cyf.

ISBN: 0-86381-721-1

Cover design: Sian Parri

Logo design: Dylan Williams

First published in 2005 by
Carreg Gwalch Cyf., 12 Iard yr Orsaf, Llanrwst,
Wales LL26 0EH
01492 642031 01492 641502
books@carreg-gwalch.co.uk
website: www.carreg-gwalch.co.uk

Supported by an 'Arts for All' Lottery grant from the Arts Council of Wales

Contents

Glyn Jones (1905-95)

Glyn Jones was born on 28 Februay 1905 in Merthyr Tydfil, Glamorgan, and attended Cyfarthfa High School in the town. Educated at St Paul's College, Cheltenham, he became a teacher at a slum school in Cardiff, where his experience of his pupils' poverty affected him deeply. Despite not being eligible for military call-up, in 1942 he registered as a conscientious objector to war on Christian pacifist grounds, and was duly dismissed from his post at Allensbank School. From 1952 until his retirement he taught at Glantaf County School in Whitchurch, Cardiff. He died at his home on 10 April 1995.

Although he spoke Welsh, Glyn Jones was unable to write creatively in it because, as he pointed out in his autobiography, *The Dragon Has Two Tongues* (1968), he had received a wholly English education at Cyfarthfa. As an adult, however, he read a great deal of Welsh literature, translated Welsh poetry into English and was happy to allow its metrics to influence his own writing, usually with pleasing results. His prose is as highly wrought and as full of vivid images as his verse.

He began as a short-story writer with the publication of *The Blue Bed* (1937), followed by *The Water Music* (1944). Lyrical, mysterious, comic and often grotesque, these stories deal for the most part with village life in Merthyr or in rural Carmarthenshire, where his family had its roots in the district of Llansteffan. His lifelong Christianity was fundamental to his vision: his fiction abounds with characters who, for all their shortcomings, are nevertheless drawn with compassion, generosity and love.

In his poem 'Merthyr', Glyn Jones wrote, 'I fancy words', and his gift for 'logopoeic dance' is evident in all his writing. His first collection, *Poems* (1939), displays his pleasure in music and colour (he had once thought of becoming a painter), while *The Dream of Jake Hopkins* (1954), originally written for radio, shows his technical virtuosity. He continued to write verse well into old age and his *Selected Poems: Fragments and Fictions* (1988) includes some of his finest work. A selection of his translations from Welsh folk-verses appeared as *A People's Poetry* in 1997 and in his *Collected Poems.*

Glyn Jones also wrote three novels: *The Valley, The City, The Village* (1956), *The Learning Lark* (1960), and *The Island of Apples* (1965). The last-named, his most important prose-work, weaves realism with fantasy and, like many of his stories, has a boy-narrator; it is set in a fictionalized Merthyr and uses the myth of Afallon to explore adolescent romanticism and the pain of its loss.

Esyllt ferch Brychan

As he climbs down our hill, my kestrel rises,
Steering in silence up from five empty fields,
A smooth sun brushed brown across his shoulders,
Floating in wide circles, his warm wings stiff.
Their shadows cut; in new soft orange hunting-boots
My lover crashes through the snapping bracken.

The still gorse-hissing hill burns, brags gold broom's
Outcropping quartz; each touched bush spills dew.
Strangely last moment's parting was never sad,
But unreal, like my promised years; less felt
Than this intense and silver snail calligraphy
Scrawled here in the sun across these stones.

Why have I often wanted to cry out
More against his going when he has left my flesh
Only for the night? When he has gone out
Hot from my mother's kitchen, and my combs
Were on the table under the lamp, and the wind
Was banging the doors of the shed in the yard.

Marwnad

The little oil lamp burns between us;
It is made of blue glass;
Beside the bare table we sit waiting
For the night to pass.

In the other room, through the open door,
I can see him lying dead,
With his pit-clothes folded where they dropped
them
Beside the bed.

His mother watches the fleece of flame
That grows over the embers
Weeping softly for this, and those other griefs
She half remembers.

My cheeks are dry for you, my man,
But you know what's for me –
Even now I am wondering when my pains
Will come upon me.

Dock

Big sidings by the swing-bridge have black tons
Of trucked rock packed in twenty rows, sun-
slavered
Coal converged upon the setting sun.
A black rat swims across the brass canal.

The sky tilts suddenly, its sleety herringbone
Of pouring rain spills thick across the dock,
Shags up the furry liner's side, its blurred
Black iron cliff immense above the dock-wall;
Pelts the sheety concrete, sprawls its gusty
growths,
Its hiss of cold grey grass across the tingling streets.

The gold coal-owner's daughter saves her hennaed
Hooks of hair, ducks pippin-breasted, slim grey-
Squirrelled, spindle-heeled, beneath some
Broker's porch; two big coal-trimmers, night-shift
Candle-pounds tucked dry, get after her.
One grins, 'God lummy Charlie,' and is silent.

Only one watcher herring-gull, turning
High up above the wetted town, sticks out,
His windy shoulder skilful in a storm
He saw ruled blue behind the Islands hours back.

Scene

This is the scene, let me unload my tongue,
Discharge perhaps some dirty water from my
chest.

The north swells, bunioned with Pumlumon,
whose
Side leaks water like some rusty old
Boiler's brickwork; his bleeding plait; cars at
spring-tides
Line the river roads, switch headlights on, stroke
The stopped tide with car beams, finger the night
bore.
That's Severn. Southward, beyond the bottled
Channel,
England, Somerset, like foreign parts, and west,
John Masefield's notchy water, Cardigan Bay.

Circuited thus my crumbled country lies.

The flat eyes of the Pembroke hawks discern
Zigzag coast-cliffs, three-ply islands, black rocks
Stuck bad-toothed and edgy from blue-bag sea.
(One night not pinholed by a single star,
I lay half-frozen in the light-house field
And heard the fighting gulls, the prow-wash tide,
My body swept with big beams swung from
Strumble Head;)

Vine-veins of rivers flourish everywhere;
Some plains, paint-blistered into bolt-head hills;
The cloud-clawed mountains; prick-lark, a
darkened star,
Drops, sees like a batter Beacon peaks,
Stiff, rough, stirred, gone solid-hard, rush up,
Fan Lleia, Fan Gihirich, Pen y Fan
A wool road winding white along each pass.

You men who bus or walk for mart-day towns,
Bear baskets full containing fish or rabbits,
Are river-limers, clubbers of salmon,
I might have been, and liked it, born like you
Westward, or north, beyond the crooked coalfields.
But night on the Valleys and my first star stood
Voluble above those Beacon peaks,
Gesticulating like a tick-tack man.

Standing now where that birth-star was eloquent
I see my bitter county dawn between
My hands, I grieve above five valleys leaning
Suppliant against my unstruck rock.
The cream rose blushing sweet and scarlet stares
Back along the barren pink-hooked stem.
I hear my heart speak to the bleaky sky,
Coal and the Valleys were my lucky egg,
As though some bird should scribble his short
song.
I feel the mobbing flowers hug my feet;

The winds descend about my body, hoarse
As a garment, and my lonely burning flesh
Smokes up this sky-hook like a plunging fish.
Proudly I hail this pale past-sailing sun.

Island

The tiny cream-bricked lighthouse on the hill
Glitters, seeing all and this. The island grass
Is silent and pale green, the high dry tide
Deep blue-wood water, smooth and shadowless,
Smooth to the white upright collar of the cliff.
One tealeaf swimmer swims that dusty sea.
Radiant and woollen gold, the sun sees too
The tilted gold-browed moon bent on the little park
Whose paths are heaped with snow, or burnt-wood
black.
Over the velvet railings of the pond
A white-edged hunchback feeds a swan with cake.
The fancy bridge has bamboo legs, combs back
The river's long blue hair; and on its hump a boy,
Bald-headed, wearing lemon boots, leans back
Flying the fish-kite, while his Jessie sits
On gaudy grass to touch the raisin tree.
Pass, doves, and pass, you coal-flanked elephant,
Jessie's tall corn-coloured tree;
Make with your crimson satan-satin sash
Towards the glittering lighthouse, where the glass
Flashes its little lightnings to the sun.

Town

And he watched from the cat-eyed bell-turret
The sea-smokes, and the flat town under them,
The sheety roofs, half-blessed by this faint blue
Glove of mist, gently touching the Welsh flanks
Of distant hills with long divided fingers;
And the dome-leads, and the shining copper cocks
Circling the milky bulk of tomb-like towered clock.
Coal-smoke steamed across the lizard-crested
Ploughland of the near streets, and roofs
Patterned with a formal dew of slums.
St Peter's pinnacle was a sharpened pencil,
Towered Trinity a four-fanged tooth reversed,
St Paul's a ball and cross beneath a crowsfoot
Lightning conductor. Southwards, towards
The edgeless sea, six infant orange stacks
Issued in a row their sheepish smokes,
A soft snort of grey, like human breath.
Huge and brilliant on their snowy tower,
Towards the wipe of sun, gleamed the brass numbers
And the sworded face of that gigantic four-faced clock,
The burning morning oval of its rim.
Great cats dangle on the castle wicks,
The lemon lions of the marquis stir
Under the menace of black-breasted clouds.

Stars

Stepping out at night expecting rain
Before the cold hostility of darkness,
I recoil confronted by the menace
Of the gathering stars. They stand out
In brilliance from their ambush, one by one –
Surrounded I surrender.

From The Dream of Jake Hopkins

JAKE

(Slowly)

Here I stand, a middle-aged master,
My hair like tow and my face like plaster,
Awaiting my class – and awaiting disaster.

This is my register, where crimson rain rages,
The ink-strokes a downpour no thinking
assuages,
For those who've been absent, I must work up a
warning.

The bell-tower booms for the school-day's
beginning.
But I hear in its thunders an under-bell tolling
For the heart in me dead, and diurnally dying.

Here I sit staring, a has-been teacher,
Behind my moustache, like a straw-haired
Nietzsche.
All is vanity, I say with the preacher.

The slow and the skittish, my forty boys enter,
The smart and the smoker, the hard to
remember,
The coltish, the doltish – my mask looks like
murder!

(Briskly)

All stand, all still, all silent, all sit.
You mustn't smile, you mustn't sneeze, you
mustn't scratch, you mustn't spit.
Keep clean, keep cool, keep sweet, keep still.
Don't be late, don't be lazy, don't be lousy, don't
be ill.

Never mitch, never moan, never cry, never quit.
You'll be famous, you'll be wealthy, you'll be
worthy, you'll be IT!
ALL SIT!

(Slowly)

Here I scowl on a sad Monday morning
Cross as cats'-cradles – but my Bashan-bull
bawling
Is counterfeit only – the soul of me's yawning.

(Brisker)

But here comes my headmaster, the great I AM,
His leering visage brazen as Birmingham,
Like a fanged grin off the roof of Notre Dame.

HEADMASTER

(Sotto voce)

I am the sole headmaster of this school.
I know that Hopkins here thinks I'm a fool.

Fool or no fool – this much must be said –
Hopkins is still a teacher – while I'm a head.

(Aloud)

Good morning, Mr Hopkins. Good morning, all
you boys.
Now get on nicely with your work, and get on
without noise.
Revise your money tables, and length, and
avoirdupois.

Now, Mr Hopkins, may I see your weekly
record book?
Is that your yearly syllabus? I'd like to have a
look.
When you mark your dinner register, I hope
you check the cash,
Because though these boys can't do their sums –
they'll cheat you in a flash.
This lad I see is absent – you should have put a
dash.
I expect you've marked your papers, and got
your lists prepared,
Of the terminal exams, to show how every boy
has fared,
And drawn nice red-ink brackets on them
where a place is shared?
Now your file of record cards – I very much
deplore

That my teachers look on filling them as
something of a bore.
I hope you'll do your forty, Mr H., by half past
four.
Then from this left-hand column – could you
calculate for me
All those boys who'll be thirteen plus in
nineteen sixty-three?
And the boys who write left-handed, for filling
form C3.
That only leaves the savings. Is there anything
I've missed?
Oh yes, the number present – and the
requisition list –
And a list of all addresses – and the ages in a list –
And a list of all boys absent – and a list of every
list
That you've listed in your thirty years of list
begetting list
List, list, list, list, list list, list . . .

JAKE

A scowl and a bawl and the boys drop their larking,
And attend to this rigmarole, register marking.
Twice a day they and I must endure this clerking.

A is for Andrews, who climbs a club table
And sings every night there in heavenly treble;
No wonder his peaked face is pale as a pebble.

B is for Billo, in cassock and puttees;
He terrifies all who might jeer at these tatties
By his lunatic laughs as he beats up his butties.

C is for Claude with the kick of a broncho;
D is a Dai-cap who always lies doggo;
And **E**ddie's a blusher who'll sing nothing solo
Though his notes are as sweet as the voice of bel
canto.

Fred climbed the pylon that holds the high tension;
He saw the red notice but paid no attention.
Now Fred's a peg-leg, it's important to mention.

Gwyn's a bird-watcher, and **H**arry a smiler;
Id is my top boy, and **J**im a half-miler;
Ken, in no underclothes, is tough as a tiler.

What I note in young **L**en is his love for a
Woodbine,
And soaped hair combed up like the blades of a
turbine.

Murphy's home is a ruin, with one double-bedder
For swarms of young Murphys, the younger the
madder.
Now their stairs have collapsed they go up on a
ladder.

N – Neville sells newspapers, knows all the angles.
Why is he wearing green gloves with bright
spangles?

Oliver also – he leans out to starboard
Through hawking round newsprint for Gulp, Son
and Cardboard.

P – Peter, big-bosomed – that swollen pullover
Holds comforts for conies – clean shavings and
clover.

Quentin's our fatty, our fool and first-aider;
When he treated Len's cut he bound up the wrong
finger.

Fifty lengths of the baths are no burden
To neatest and sweetest of swimmers, **R**iordan.
But he's clumsy in classrooms as gulls in a garden.

Stan has been fighting – his eye and its fellow,
Like the signs of the AA, are black and chrome
yellow,
Though his nose remains trim as the nose of
Novello.

In his daydreams **T**om hands around jewels and
sables
To a lure of Lamours and a glamour of Grables;

But it's strong horses' work to teach Tom his times-
tables.

Ungoed too is a dreamer – that flat medallion
Of face hides a victor astride a white stallion,
Or a prince who elopes with a girl and a galleon.

V is for Vernon and Verdun his brother
Spoilt by a late start and too-loving mother.

And **W**at's granny Williams is just as adoring;
She keeps a sly brothel and lives on the whoring,
But instead of being spicy her talk is plain boring.

The keen and the cosy, the lout and the limber,
The blond and orbicular, the eager for slumber,
XYZ are the others who make up the number.

PART 3

MRS OWEN: Why isn't Jake a Head?
MRS BOWEN: Why *isn't* he a Head?
MRS OWEN: He's too much of a churchman.
MRS BOWEN: He's too much of a red.
MRS COHEN: He makes blots on his register and
rubs them out with bread!

MRS OWEN: Will Jake *ever* be a Head?
MRS BOWEN: He'll *never* be a Head.
MRS OWEN: Yet he knows those Latin poets.

MRS BOWEN: Knows the Greek ones too, it's
said.
MRS COHEN: He ought to know old Alderman
Cadwaladar instead!

MRS OWEN: Why isn't Jake a boss?
MRS BOWEN: Why *isn't* he a boss?
MRS OWEN: Some say he'd make a mess of it.
MRS BOWEN: Some say he's quite a loss.
MRS COHEN: Some say as far as Headships go
he doesn't care a toss.

MRS OWEN: Jake's not fit to be a Head.
MRS BOWEN: He's not at all well-bred.
MRS OWEN: He lets the boys do anything.
MRS BOWEN: Is he quite right in the head?
MRS COHEN: I heard those Baboon Terrace louts
locked him in his shed.

MRS OWEN: I can't see Jake a Head.
MRS BOWEN: He'll *never* be a Head.
MRS OWEN: He spites the other teachers.
MRS BOWEN: Once to spite the Head
He went home Monday playtime
and spent the week in bed.

MRS OWEN: Why isn't Jake a boss?
MRS BOWEN: As a Head he'd be imposs.

You never know what Jake will say
Once you get him cross.

MRS COHEN: He called those Baboon Terrace people muck and moral dross.

MRS OWEN: Would Jake ever make a Head?

MRS BOWEN: An awful dance he's led;
They say he started nature study –
Now all his fish are dead –
The boys used marking-ink and turned his aquarium water red.

MRS OWEN: Why isn't he a Head?

MRS BOWEN: Jake will never be a Head.

MRS OWEN: He's not a faithful churchman.

MRS BOWEN: He's never been a red.

MRS COHEN: He's never joined the Party club –
is he quite right in the head?

MRS OWEN: Why isn't Jake a boss?

MRS BOWEN: He'll never be a boss.

MRS OWEN: They say that every day in school
He takes a little doss.

MRS COHEN: But no-one can call him the rolling stone that never gathers moss.

REES ART: After all these years Jake's bound to regard his teaching with abhorrence.

PREECE CHEM: Why didn't he start to write sexy books like that poet D.H. Lawrence

Who began, like Jake, in the Band
of Hope, but rose above his station
By composing books with dirty
talk about high-toned fornication?

THOS. FRENCH: Or why not follow Mallarmé,
whose poems he goes on learning
When he hardly knows if murder
is meant or only a cart-wheel
turning.

JONES LATIN: Jake says though ambiguity is very
much to his fancy
He fears the Frenchman's line
would mean – sharing a dentist's
doxy.

MORGAN MATHS: Why doesn't he write like
Milton then, Tractates on
Education,
His rhythms concern the fitting a
man for any job in the nation?

PARRY ENGLISH: One thing he lacks – those
Phillips boys – there's no-one upon
whose breeches
He can dithyramb his rhythms out
and yet ignore the screeches.

PREECE CHEM: Then what about that James Joyce man – they say he too was a teacher
Like Milton, Lawrence and Mallarmé – couldn't Jake think up some feature
To put our school on the map of fame and get himself some glory?

OMNES: Reading the classics is one thing – writing's a different story.

JAKE

Here I stand, a middle-aged teacher,
Behind my moustache like a straw-haired Nietzsche.
All is vanity, I say with the Preacher.

Here I stand, a middle-aged master.
When my heart went to stone and my world to disaster
I repaired my glasses with surgical plaster.

Easter

Morning in the honey-months, the star
Of annunciation still lit in the sky,
Upon me fell the heavy unpinned hair
Of apple, perfumed, almond, pear,
With dawn-chorus, dewfall, and the incarnate
Promise of the primrose flesh in bloom.
Leaving the morning garden, I sought the room,
The bedside of a woman winsome to me
Once, though old, clean in her white cap, comely
In candle-light, or the green shine of stars.

In death's stink now, with tears I watch her, old
And hideous in her dying – bitterly
She moans, her face death-dark, her tangled hair
Tortured behind her little rolling head.
She wakes a moment, calming our kindling room,
Opens untroubled eyes and lifting up
Bone arms like glistening sticks, prays for the droll
Child of her weeping sailor. Anguish returns;
Again she moans – it is the grave-bound flesh
That grieves – but soon now must remission come
Upon the agony of this endured embrace,
Soon must the flesh rot in its stony bed.

Now, with a burning in the east, the breeze
Curves across the young cheek of the day;
Soon shall the thrush be at his crowing point,

Frailer than filigree the stems begin to bud;
Soon over grooved fields shall grow the soft
Plush-pile of the grass-like wheat, the green
Velvety nap of springing corn burst forth –
Soon, soon, the doors of every grave shall open
And the light of dawn shall shine upon the dead.

Again

Lamplight from our kitchen window-pane
Shines out on the leaves of the little apple-tree
Dripping in the rain.

Inside the warm room, those two women together
Cleaning the brass candlesticks in silence
Are my daughter and my mother.

She has become a woman to me, my daughter,
Her dress heavy with her breasts, her arms heavy;
She is desired now, she is a lover.

But what will have come to her, and been hers,
Her crooked hands idle on the table
And her feet slow on the stairs?

Her granny, tired out, her mouth dropped open,
Sits with her eyes shut, facing the lamplight.
She has seen so much happen.

Shall my daughter too run through the streets to
the pit-head,
And stand cold among the women crowding the
gateway,
And see the young men brought up dead?

Merthyr

Lord, when they kill me, let the job be thorough
And carried out behind that county borough
Known as Merthyr, in Glamorganshire.
It would be best if it could happen, Sir,
Upon some great green roof, some Beacon slope
Those monstrous clouds of childhood slid their soap
Snouts over, into the valley. The season,
Sir, for shooting, summer; and love the reason.
On that hill, varnished in the glazing tide
Of evening, stand me, with the petrified
Plantations, the long blue spoonful of the lake,
The gold stook-tufted acres without break
Below me, and the distant corduroy
Glass of the river – which, a mitching boy,
I fished – flowing as though to quench
The smouldering coalfield in its open trench
Of steamy valley, fifteen miles away.
Here, Sir, are more arrangements for that day:-
Lay me, lead-loaded, below the mourning satin
Of some burnt-out oak; the skylark's chirpy Latin
Be my *'Daeth yr awr'*; gather the black
Flocks for bleaters – sweet grass their ham – upon the back
Of lonely Fan Gihirych; let night's branchy tree
Glow with silver-coated planets over me.

And yet, sometimes, I can't help wondering;
Is this rather posh poetic death the thing,
After all, for somebody like me? I realize
I have a knack for telling bardic lies,
To say I see in some protean hill
A green roof, ship's prow or an eagle's bill;
To claim the mountain stream for me's as clear
As flowing gin, and yet as brown as beer.
I fancy words, some critics praise me for
A talent copious in metaphor.
But this my gift for logopœic dance
Brothers, I know, a certain arrogance
Of spirit, a love of grandeur, style and dash,
Even vain-glory, the gaudiest panache,
Which might impel to great rascality
A heedless heart. This glorying in all
Created things, the golden sun, the small
Rain riding in the wind, the silvery shiver
Of the dawn-touched birches, and the chromium river,
Innocent itself, has yet calamitous
And wilful pride for child and famulus.
And thus I see the point when puritan
Or mystic poet harried under ban
Sensual nature, earth, sea and firmament;
I apprehend some strain of what they meant,
And look at nature with a wary eye.
Sir, that death I sought was pure effrontery.

Lord, when they kill me, let the job be thorough
And carried out *inside* that county borough
Known as Merthyr, in Glamorganshire,
A town easy enough to cast a slur
Upon, I grant. Some cyclopean ball
Or barn-dance, some gigantic free-for-all,
You'd guess, had caused her ruins, and those slums –
Frightening enough, I've heard, to daunt the bums –
Seem battered wreckage in some ghastly myth,
Some nightmare of the busting aerolith.
In short, were she a horse, so her attackers
Claim, her kindest destination were the knackers.
Yet, though I've been in Dublin, Paris, Brussels,
London, of course, too, I find what rustles
Oftenest and scentiest through the torpid trees
Of my brain-pan, is some Merthyr-mothered breeze,
Not dreams of them – a zephyr at its best
Acting on arrogance like the alkahest.

An object has significance or meaning
Only to the extent that human feeling
And intellect bestow them. All that sensational news
The heart hears, before she starts to bruise
Herself against the universe's rocky rind,
Is what she treasures most – the sight of wind
Fretting a great beech like an anchored breaker;
The vale, pink-roofed at sunset, a heavenly acre

Of tufted and irradiated toothpaste; the moon
Glistening sticky as snail-slime in the afternoon;
Street-papers hurdling, like some frantic foal,
The crystal barriers of squalls; the liquid coal
Of rivers; the hooter's loud liturgic boom;
Pit-clothes and rosin fragrant in a warm room –
Such sensations deck a ruinous scene
(To strangers) with tinsel, scarlet, spangles, green,
Gold, ribbons, and the glare of pantomime's
Brilliancy in full floods, foots and limes.

But far more than the scene, the legendary
Walkers and actors of it, the memory
Of neighbours, worthies, relatives,
Their free tripudiation, is what gives
That lump of coal that Shelley talks about
Oftenest a puff before it quite goes out.
My grandfather's fantastic friends, old Siôn
O Ferthyr, occultist, meddler with the unknown –
(The spirits in malevolence one night
Nigh strangled him, but sobered Siôn showed fight!)
My grandfather himself, musician, bard,
Pit-sinker, joker, whom the Paddys starred
As basser for their choir – so broken out!
My undersized great granny, that devout
Calvinist, with mind and tongue like knives;
The tall boys from Incline Top, and those boys' wives;

The tailor we believed a Mexican,
A rider of the prairies; Dr Pan
Jones (he it was who gave my father
The snowy barn-owl) Bishop – *soi-disant* rather;
Refined Miss Rees; Miss Thomas ditto; Evan
Davies, and the Williamses from Cefn.
Sir, where memories, dense as elephant
Grass, of these swarm round, in some common
pant
Or hilltop lay me down; may the ghostly breeze
Of their presence be all my obsequies;
Not sheep and birds about me, but lively men,
And dead men's histories, O Lord. Amen.

Cwmcelyn

His wings blissful in a silent drumming
Of beautiful sunlight, the buzzard. Below him,
The estuary; below him the hills,
Green fields with the hay gone; the cornfields,
Silent and sunburnt encampments
Of wheat-stooks; below him the tranquil
River, gently heaving the mirrors
Afloat on her surface; below him
These woods, where flashes the grey pigeon,
White in the paint of her flying.
Below him Cwmcelyn, the farm.

Now the griefs of that homestead are mine.
Drunken, in anger, or passion,
Dejected, trampling this warm web-work of shadow
Between village and farm, my blood,
Through long generations, bore their flesh.
Let me not, in the repose of this sunlight,
Tranquil on fields and on heaving estuary, see
Their symbol and image; or falsify
Toiling and poverty, rebellion
And bitterness of theirs to a pastoral
Heaven. Defilement was theirs, and folly,
Suffering, questioning and death. And yet
Between them and the Eternal, a harmony.

Soon shall I leave these swarthy cornfields,
  The dawdling gull, and the grave river, for
  The acrid city, where the body of the burnt
Saint smoked in its unavailing martyrdom;
Where now the sacrifice of love is not enjoined;
  For the talk, for the belittling fool,
  For the annihilation, for no God,
No king, no shrine, no sanctuary.
Whose is the name to which every knee
  In that city's empty-hearted wilderness
  Shall bow? Ghostly reapers of Cwmcelyn,
You arraign them the demoniac folly,
The soul's dissonance, and the despair.

Watcher

At the end of the field here I have waited, and am
waiting;
The eastern clouds behind the trees are soaked in
blackness,
And stars come out and ripen in the clear stretches
of sky.
How long shall I wait for your coming out of the
waters?

The black sea beyond the field is smooth as a river,
And the red reflection of a buoy-light writhes there;
Far on the left, fifty fields away,
The lighted village stretches out like a glowing
filament.

When shall I see you coming up golden before me?
Coming warm and full between sea and sky,
With the heavens, moon of the south, golden-green
about you;
When shall I see you rising warm out of the
waters?

Comrades

As I gazed across the mountains
  Thunders prowled the dusty plain,
And on its dust the jetty fountains
  Squandered gems. The land seemed Spain.

I laughed to watch my comrade glancing
  Through his verse of rubric red,
In sun and dusty jewels dancing,
  A snow-dove circling round his head!

Faint wood-peckering! Round him gusty
  Sea-guns flickered. Rose-red fans
Of fire roaring, vast and dusty,
  Thundered a darkness that was man's.

Silence, death, beneath the cloud-dome.
  I saw the radiant round moon swerve
Her vast glow on the gold transparent
  Bubble of that glassy curve,

Where in moonlight he lay sleeping;
  A corpse-rick was my comrade's bed;
His gems were tears of the weeping,
  And on his breast his dove lay dead.

I swooned to see that moonlit body,
   And soon the giant earth-worm wave
Well-fed from the bones of beauty
   Magnified upon his grave.

I bled, I woke upon the mountains.
   Did I see his snow-dove leave her cave?
On the sunlit plain were those his fountains
   That gushed new jewels round his grave?

Ambush

Midnight, and the new moon sunk.
Into the wood the soldier peers.
In dread and dark the forest seems
An army resting on its spears.

Oh, hostile spears, spare this boy,
In anguish now, before the fight,
Butchering fears who find his heart
Their forest and their moonless night.

He hears the crash, and sees the glare
On rocking trees and quaking land.
One dewdrop, in a gentle curve,
Falls, a soft jewel, upon his hand.

A new throb thunders through his heart;
He lies in stupor at this sign;
In death and dark the eternal pause
Is proffered now, like bread and wine.

And now, with ghostly eucharist,
He feels the heavenly hungers fed;
For him, on grave and heaving ground,
The auguries of love are spread.

The seagull

(after the Welsh of Dafydd ap Gwilym)

Gracing the tide-warmth, this seagull,
The snow-semblanced, moon-matcher,
The sun-shard and sea-gauntlet
Floating, the immaculate loveliness.
The feathered one, fishfed, the swift-proud,
Is buoyant, breasting the combers.
Sea-lily, fly to this anchor to me,
Perch your webs on my hand.
You nun among ripples, habited
Brilliant as paper-work, come.
Girl-glorified you shall be, pandered to,
Gaining that castle mass, her fortalice.
Scout them out, seagull, those glowing battlements,
Reconnoitre her, the Eigr-complexioned.
Repeat my pleas, my citations, go
Girlward, gull, where I ache to be chosen.
She solus, pluck up courage, accost her,
Stress your finesse to the fastidious one;
Use honeyed diplomacy, hinting
I cannot remain extant without her.
I worship her, every particle worships!
Look, friends, not old Merddin, hot-hearted,
Not Taliesin the bright-browed, beheld
The superior of this one in loveliness.
Cypress-shapely, but derisive beneath

Her tangled crop of copper, gull,
O, when you eye all Christendom's
Loveliest cheek – this girl will bring
Annihilation upon me, should your answer
Sound, gull, no relenting note.

Dawn trees

Morning of cold green, grape and the golden
  Water-candles, crystal in soft stars, and
The fragile bangle of a new moon's milk.
Sun lights the blue palm, rooted upon the
  Shores of her long blue pool of shadow.

Old man in mourning, his knee-bone crooked,
bows,
  Beneath his burden, green leaves and black
wine.

Breeze stirs the olive, the great grey wrestler
  Hurls off his invisible adversary.

Now is the juniper's green breeze called joy.

Morning

On the night beach, quiet beside the blue
Bivouac of sea-wood, and fresh loaves, and the
Fish baking, the broken ghost, whose flesh burns
Blessing the dark bay and the still mast-light,
Shouts, 'Come'.
                    A naked man on deck who heard
Also cockcrow, turning to the pebbles, sees
A dawn explode among the golden boats,
Pulls on his sea-plaid, leaps into the sea.

Wading the hoarfrost meadows of that fiord's
Daybreak, he, hungering fisherman, forgets
Cockcrow tears, dark noon, dead god, empty cave,
All those mountains of miraculous green
Light that swamped the landing-punt, and kneels,
Shivering, in a soaked blouse, eating by the
Blue blaze the sweet breakfast of forgiveness.

Y Ddraig Goch

The Red Dragon flies aloft, behind him burns
The vast thinned out flame of golden sunrise.
The city floats up in silver. Venus spills on the sea.

The Red Dragon waves over the blue carapace of roofs.
Breakers of the sun's illumination enter through windows,
They appear as gleaming scabs on rococo decorations.

The Red Dragon leaps up. Swallows are elegant stumblers.
The golden string of the sun is dabbled in the bay.
Why is there no dancing among the cancerous?

The Red Dragon heaves joyfully in the suburban summer.
A disorder of golden chains in tangled silence loads the trees.
Coal is no less intractable in the two-foot seams.

The Red Dragon waves on high; once a dawn fire of twigs,
The hot sun now glints like tin on the green lagoon.

The old language only is heard from the
sunburnt beachfuls.

The Red Dragon flies forward; every dawn
dewdrop is a peacock.
The great gold sun floats awash in the bay. Only
Welsh is exchanged
On Sunday beaches hideous with shit and
transistors.

The Red Dragon triumphs over the silver-
backed smokes.
Until the city is a cairn, the language of
Llanrhaeadr and Pantycelyn
Shall be used for the utterance of her cruelty, her
banalities, her lies.

The Red Dragon leaps above the inherited gaol.
Sunbeams, incandescent up to the shoulder, probe
into darkened cells.
What cause has conscience not to render the
dragon his coinage?

The Red Dragon leaps, his claws and belly-mail
are black.
The prisoner stares at the glowing ingot of his
sunbeam.
Why should not bombs bring the paradise of
daffodils at nine a penny?

The Red Dragon leaps like a demented acrobat.
To the convicted his comrades are a meadow of
green grass,
He objects to their being eaten equally by goats
and unicorns.

The Red Dragon flies in green rain falling cold.
The sweet land, tender and fruitful under the
native foot,
Has long been the property of random
foreigners.

The Red Dragon flies over valleys for sale.
The Welsh
Mountains, loveliest under the suns of heaven,
Are the inheritance of generations of native
expropriators.

The Red Dragon flies on every building. How
can we, like the bullet-
Spattering Mexican, kneel down and give a
scooped up
Handcupful of Welsh soil Zapata's kiss of
ecstasy?

Bindweed

Suddenly the scent of bindweed in the warm
lane
And the smoking sea of remembering him bursts
open
Upon its rocks, its snow-dust wets the sun.

The heavy scent of bindweed brings only
sorrow.
Grey gull-flocks puffed over waves disintegrate
like gunsmoke.
Storm-sodden crags are not colder than my
heart.

Bindweed is the scent of heavy remembering.
Beyond the window – the great ocean in its bed.
I am alone. In the past Gwynn was with me.

The scent of bindweed drifts like childhood
remembered.
Meshed white on green is the great wave's
polished incurve.
Bullets that took Gwynn were already in flight.

Cruel the sweet scent of innocent bindweed.
Winds tear off the tide's skin in one brandished
fleece.
Gwynn died. Happiness is irrational.

Bindweed now in this lane, then in that sea-
garden.
Waves everywhere throw anguished arms around
rocks.
The comforter in his comforting is not
comforted.

Sweet bindweed was heavy in that August
garden.
The grey sea stiffens and sinks to a slab of iron.
How is it the heart dead as its quick can suffer?

Where all were good to me, God knows

Seeing the block of flats, I remember
The meadows under them, where Jones the
Stoning's
Skewbald cart-horse would walk in sunshine
Camouflaged conspicuous as a tank,
Among the fluid swallows,
And the Jones's white-washed house,
And their long garden with the door in the wall,
In at which squat Russ and I floated and, through
Subaqueous gloom of their glass trees, out
On to their sunlit lawn, vast and glowing.
'Welcome, come in, my boy,' said Mr Jones
– A shy man, he was never in the handshake
First to remit the pressure – adding
'zzz', when he saw there were two of us.
God bless much overfed, norfolk-suited,
Green-stockinged, yellow-booted Mr Jones
– Destined for his nest, must be, I thought, that fluff
Moustache – his high collar, his high colour
Glassy, tight over his shining head
The polished membrane of his tarry hair.
And his crippled Philip also, rowdiest
Hunchback goalie in the game – I remember
His brown hair-helmet (in sunlight the red
Gravy of sea-iron), his sad faces inked
On finger-nails, his nutmeg freckling,
The feel of crutch-pads warm from his armpits.

We played cards and ate apples,
While seating Mr Jones, dumb talker,
Witty listener, sat watching us before
His red bed of flat sun-gulper tulips,
And the sun-soaked wall where deep udders
Of shadow hung down darkening the brickwork –
Beaming, his fat hand nursing his fat fist.

A raft of starlings exploded off the grass,
A full thrush hopped heavily with long
Kangaroo hops down the lawn and slowly
Mrs Jones followed, long-frocked from the
dazzling house.
God bless his beautiful Mrs Jones also,
Her drake-head-green gown, her broad-brimmed
hat, her cool
Face gold, radiant in lawn-reflected amber,
Her smile a mirror in which I smiled to see
Myself always clever, beautiful and good,
And before which off-white-handed Russ blushed
Into his shirt, and his aitches were the aitches,
Soon, of a boy who never sounded aitches.
Mr Jones's face turned sharp out of shadow
Towards her, smiling, and some long curled tendril,
Some hot nostril hair, suddenly lit up red,
Glowed in sunlight like a burning filament.

All are dead, Jones the Stoning, Mrs Jones,
Philip, Russ, the charm, the tenderness, the glow.
Evening drops a vast sun into sunset
Where it smoulders swollen, boiling behind
The flats – once the great cart-horses pounded on
Pavings of those night-fall-slated meadows,
Where grey Danter, too, the Jones's pig-headed
Pony stood asleep beneath the burnt-out tree.
God bless beautiful flats also, I suppose.
Lights go on in windows. People live in them
And great stars flash among vanished branches
And night-owls call from elms no longer there.

Goodbye, what were you?

At the voice of the mother on a warm hearth,
   Dark and firelit, where the hobbed kettle
                                                            crinkled
In the creak and shudder of the rained-on window,
   This world had its beginning
And was here redeemed.

All in that kitchen's warmth, that mother's glow,
   Was blessèd, nothing was abandoned.
There God's boy was born, loving, by lantern light,
   His church built of the breathing of cattle;
Before nightfall all lost in prowling woods were
                                                            home;
   To the dying in cactus land a hand came full of
                                                            rain;
Here a child wept repentant into a Father's breast,
   Warm for his childish tears, not bright with
                                                            stars,
Or filled with his suffering that mother's arms
   And in the shawls of her prayers and kisses
                                                            slept.

In the kitchen shadow and flicker and warmth,
   And the deafening storm, thickening hair by
                                                            hair
Its blinding pelt of tempest on the window panes.

War and peace

Under the vast burning-glass of the Second
World War's hatred, I walked dying down
Bridge Street, Pontypridd, and flung out suddenly

Wide wings, are they, soaring in some torrid gyre –
Great boughs, exultant, naked in the gale –
This glow, is it rosier than the low sun's
Firelight, jammed ruby in autumn sumacs –
Coiled, am I, in the hot armpit of the hills,
Warming my orange wampum in your rays?

Through the black cloud's roof of agony, your rigid
Beams fell vertical and golden with the sheen
Of oil, fruitful upon my deserts, your broken
Milk bled, slaking the huge suck of my roots.
What happened was little enough like this.
But how could I, frightened and confused, present,
Even to those who believe and speak
The language, the meaning of *tangnefedd Duw*?

Another country

The young sycamore puts out new slender stems
Among bomb-site willowherb and white-limed
Masonry; her wax buds break, each long bead or pod,
Pinkish, packed with its tight toad's hand of leaf,
Opens in fragile emerald, but soft;
Her leaves turn, soon, solid bronze, opaque
In sunshine, metallic, sharply incised,
But breathing, tender, alive and beautiful.

The children have put a rope around her neck.

From my upstairs schoolroom window once I watched
The child run from his empty sun-baked yard
And cross the meadow, making for the dark woods.
Somewhere upon that path, that universe's
Longest voyage, from heart to heart, I stand lost,
Love's road leads back, always, here, journeys back
Towards this other mystery of my self,
While the child moves on beyond, exultant
And incommunicable through his dark trees –
Woods of untarnished images, perceptions
Like thunderclaps, chimeras, symbols,
Passion, terror, ecstasy, despair.

O dark impenetrable forest,
  Over whose frontiers, for what strange rituals,
Propitiation, sacrifice perhaps,
  Unfathomable ceremonials of their guilt
And innocence, do the children lead
  The doomed beauty of this bursting sycamore?

The common path

On one side the hedge, on the other the brook:
   Each afternoon I, unnoticed, passed
The middle-aged schoolmistress, grey-haired,
   Gay, loving, who went home along the path.

That spring she walked briskly, carrying her bag
   With the long ledger, the ruler, the catkin twigs,
Two excited little girls from her class
   Chattering around their smiling teacher.

Summer returned, each day then she approached
                                                  slowly,
   Alone, wholly absorbed, as though in defeat
Between water and hazels, her eyes heedless,
   Her grey face deeply cast down. Could it be
Grief at the great universal agony had begun
   To feed upon her heart – war, imbecility,
Old age, starving, children's deaths, deformities?
   I, free, white, gentile, born neither
Dwarf nor idiot, passed her by, drawing in
   The skirts of my satisfaction, on the other side.

One day, at the last instant of our passing,
   She became, suddenly, aware of me
And, as her withdrawn glance met my eyes,
   Her whole face kindled into life, I heard
From large brown eyes a blare of terror, anguished

Supplication, her cry of doom, death, despair.
And in the warmth of that path's sunshine
And of my small and manageable success
I felt at once repelled, affronted by her suffering,
The naked shamelessness of that wild despair.

Troubled, I avoided the common until I heard
Soon, very soon, the schoolmistress, not from
Any agony of remote and universal suffering
Or unendurable grief for others, but
Private, middle-aged, rectal cancer, was dead.
What I remember, and in twenty years have
Never expiated, is that my impatience,
That one glance of my intolerance,
Rejected her, and so rejected all
The sufferings of wars, imprisonments,
Deformities, starvation, idiocy, old age –
Because fortune, sunlight, meaningless success,
Comforted an instant what must not be comforted.

Nant Ceri

Blessèd were those Bowens who saw all this – viz.,
Dawn's sort of rosin glow, then the sun's red-
gold
Mountain, floating up through green, a dazzle
In windows distant from this window; masses
Of garden azaleas bloom plum-blue, porcelain,
Apricot, or their liquor, from emerald
Fogs under the iron pear boughs, glows ruby
Like jewels or lit wine; the long-tailed mountain
pony,
Milky, saddled with morning silver, wax-white
On fire-green turf her unshod hooves, munches
In this hush of mountains her black rug
Of shadow; breeze blows the green grass blaze
glossy
And bends, bows into a gentle curve, the
children's
Rope, hung from branches of the flashing
orchards;
A green moon too clouds milky as sea-glass –
Blessèd were those Bowens who saw all this
For three lifetimes and believed in God.

You, Taliesin

You, Taliesin, in the great *Addwynau*
    Of your elaborate praise,
Called over a hundred things beautiful –
    Long-maned stallions at stud,
        Silver bracelets and necklaces,
            The age of innocence,
                Charlock in young corn.

I ought perhaps to feel a little shame-faced
    At bringing into my own droned fragment of celebration
Such words and ideas as –
    Beautiful the sawn-off girder seen in the Valleys,
        Rusty, sticking sun-plastered out of the coke-ovens' brickwork;

Or, beautiful the staring old collier,
    Silent by the coal fire, too old,
        His hands on his knees,
            Cared-for and yet abandoned;
Or, beautiful the drab mining town,
    Its roofs fishskin under endless drizzle,
Where, young, I saw that politics
    Was about power, and people, and dreams.

But beautiful to me also the sea,
Which no doubt you intended to praise
Although you didn't;
Beautiful to watch her waters hurled,
A struggling mass, into a corner of the rocks;
Or to see her great waves crawling their
whitewash
Up the plastered cliff –
Withdrawing, she hangs delicately
Along the ledges of the black rock-wall
The milky vines of her foam.

Beautiful the sky, too, as you describe it,
The hot sun high at mid-day, or glowing large at
his setting;
And the smouldering of his long beams in the
sultry afternoons,
His shafts leaning up off the meadows, rigid
into the summer thunder-clouds,
Entering into some great funnel opening in those
heavens,
Sloping up in thick bundles of rods, golden and
vaporous, or flat, sliced into oblique sheets
of radiant whale-bone, or sombrely lined,
diagonal, smoky, with the black slant of
brilliant rigging.

Beautiful the night sky also,
   The clouds blown about gusty as woodsmoke
Before the beam of the moon's open doorway;
   Beautiful in some tranquil nightfall of autumn
A large wet star.

You, Taliesin, you did not proclaim –
   Any more than that the sea is beautiful –
Beautiful to be free, to be forgiven, to create.
   I sense your understanding, your expert
                                             concurrence.

Henffych, Ddafydd

Rain-bombed under boughs, I crouch
By brown housebricks in ruins.
Jewels on gossamer, gems,
A spider's net-full, glazes
With glassy lace of diamonds
The ruin's smashed window-pane –
Sparkling sea-mist's insignia,
Rain's jewelry, encrusted brooch,
Lustre of fiery crystals
Glittering in first-water gems,
Brilliants minute as mousemilk,
Diamonds glowing in long rows.

You, Dafydd, *eos Dyfed,*
To me spinther, maker, more,
Rain-finery's fisherman,
Netter of downpour's glitter.

Which side, Dafydd, did you serve,
If either? The English king's,
Like so many of your clan?
Were you some Baudelaire, skilled bard,
Indifferent agitator?
Did you glimpse, as Iolo once,
Culture's brutal nourishing,
Welshmen broken on Welsh land?
You, poet of love's contretemps,

Did you see *taeog*'s toiling,
Gross, sustaining foam-brows' grace,
Burnishing their broom-yellow?

I first read your words dazzled,
Heart's skin suddenly too small,
Merthyr's hair shirt forgotten
And that blade through my rib-cage.
In ecstasy, despairing,
A seablue road through Dyfed
I walked, the wind-current's bed.
A sea-gull, scarcely moving
Majestic sun-mantled wings,
Floated that air-flood's surface,
The turn of her perfect head
Imperious and indifferent.
'God, why shall I never show
One thing, anything, as sweet
(Beauty's adroit creators)
As her moving's mastery,
As yours of the bright image?'

Dafydd, I, one more croaker,
Admirer and lamenter,
Brought you once my clumsy songs.
I observed your moon's changes –
'Curved, yellow as candle-flame';
'White gleam your silver kingdoms';
'Ghostly, pale, demented moon,

You haunt Hafren's blue noon sky';
'You float towards black cloud-banks
The shine of your polished keel'.
Standing in your gale I watched
A shouting wind – 'With one hand
You drag off by the hair clouds
Clawing at the Beacons' scowl';
Heard too the wind's tiny whine –
'Your note sad through the conch-hole
Of the smallest blown snail-shell'.
Lit by your dawn suns I saw
The young birch of the shaved lawn –
'You gather your dark shadow
Over green grass towards you,
A dragging train of black lace,
You hang it over your arm'.

From these crude fragments you turn,
Indulgent and indifferent,
Widening your grin – clown's, *prif-fardd*'s –
On the girls, the golden wives,
The devastating daughters.
Bright sun breaks over white gulls;
Rain burns in the jewelled webs;
With dancer's delicacy
The spider paws the brickwork,
Gathering the brown ruined wall.

Birch

The young birch models in the green breeze
   The fluttering laciness of her leafy dress.
The sun's fireplace grows cold, winter comes –
   On the lawn now, alone, without a silk stitch on,
She stands each night entangling stars.
   Soon, delicately, in darkness, the snow falls;
Once more is her silver dressed in whiteness,
   In the brilliance of the milky openwork,
And in that morning splendour, radiant
   Beside the pool of the heart's troubled waters,
The lovely slut strips naked again.

Remembering Mari

Below the ward's darkening window
  I kiss the old inflamed cheek,
Hard, glassy, chill to my lips,
  And see a young woman at dusk walk
From the dark farmhouse, beside the hedge,
  While summer lightning flickers.
She crosses with the child the hill field's gloom,
  Between them the earthenware pitcher –
They bear now no thought, no knowledge,
  Of body's bliss, the agony, the squalor.
The stars burn low over the earth,
  We skirt the dark rick of kindling,
The pony's gold looms from the alders.
  Down at the sloping end of the grass
We reach the well's chill waters,
  We bury our cream under a dish of stars.
At the window the lightning's vein throbs agonised
  In the flesh of darkness, as I kiss, despairing,
For the last time, the crimson, stone-cold cheek.

After the sermon

Amen. Sunday morning sunshine and some stackyard's
Fragrance flood in at the open chapel doors;
The village worshippers stand silent, bowed, their thoughts
Groping again among their handbags, glasses, gloves;
The hoarse harmonium's pumped out benediction dies
And that sunlit Saron's boyish organist,
A grin bright on his burnt farm face, swivels
Across his bench and, on the greek-key bordered
Oilcloth of the aisle, drops to his knee,
His arms outspread. His wife, tall in the doorway,
Stands vexed and smiling in the dazzle, lowering
Their baby daughter's fidgeting boots down
To the brown oilcloth, and releases her.

The child bolts off in mindless ecstasy,
Along that rowdy aisle, heedless, blissful, intense,
And plunges, clinging, into her father's arms.
''Nhad. 'Nhad. 'Nhad'.

Perfect, that moment of his embracing her.

Perfect, when men and women, at that trivial end,
Seeing it, were swept perhaps back into some great
Engulphing ecstasy of love again, some warm remembered arms
Of flesh, mother's, lover's friend's; and those, the few,
Guiltless a moment and redeemed, did they feel,
Beyond the dazzle and the fragrance and the love,
At that embrace, about their fleeting blessedness,
The sunlit comfort of the cold eternal arms?

The Meaning of Fuchsias

The lush valley, the two golden mares
loving in the apple orchard,
The golden-maned for Gwilym, the milky one
for me,
And through those dark boughs the vast white
mansion-walls of heaven.
Why did we not hear, in that treachery
of sun-varnished windows,
Of handsome clouds, of the fragrant flesh of pears,
of gull-white moons in their eternal blue,
And pastures cast out of morning fire
everywhere brilliant as enamels,
The creeping by of our days, of time, of change –
Only the thrush's hammering of morning
in the dapples of that sunlight,
And the cupboards of the trees around us
creaking, creaking.
On the slope the still bushes stood in the sun,
staring down in silence at their shadows.
'Fuchsias,' said Gwilym, 'wild fuchsias' –
each bush of flowers
The dark glow in my mind still of lit lanterns
burning crimson through transparencies
of wine,
A new delight then, inextinguishable,
a heart's enduring wonder.

In these sleek gardens, where only meaning
has no root or blossoming,
What is it within me stares through its bars at
fuchsias,
So that I bear again the sudden burden
of my many dead,
And you, and all our darkened suns,
possess me through the doorways of my tears,
You, sanctified listener, who rode by night
your golden pony
Through the graveyard, listening,
and hearing nothing.

Envoi

Old, I watched the darling swallow families
gathering,
Their fringes perched, spaced out, along high
village wires,
Each sweet bird black, no wider than an eyelash –
why
Should these bring molten to my throat so old a
heart?

Blessing, I saw their swift flight above radiant
hayfields, it was warm
And summer then, in hundreds they wove their
invisible silkiness above
The standing hay (their weft swift, it was the
wennol of the waterside weavers),
Or they ruggered unstoppable down wings of the
building meadows,
They were reckless, their headlong speed, as though
defying calamity, rocked them – 'Be careful,
Dear things,' I wished to cry out in warning at such
consummate lunacy –
The wheezing machinery of their tiny cries the
sweetest of birdsong;
Black and white in their beauty, in their rashness
they licked out sleek wings,
They were dark, they were glossy, rigid the
symmetry of their forked tail feathers.

Now it is all over. They gather on the high wires
twittering in excitement
To be gone in this gloom. Goodbye, you were the
lovely white lilac birds,
Your flocks flying in to our wastelands trawled
here warmth
From the longed-for south, from the lands where
sunlight falls
Bright on dark skins, brilliant on the beauty of the
dappled antelope,
On olives and honey, balm, oil and barley – early
figs
Are there also and heavy gold leaking everywhere
from sunlit trees.
Goodbye, goodbye, you were about us in sunlight,
swift,
Bright as the astonishment of youthful perceptions
– lovely as glancing epiphanies
The gaiety of your visitations; and now you
prepare joyfully to leave us,
Heedless you take off for ever, you are visions and
images,
The words and their dazzle, you leave me bereft,
darling birds,
You will plunge elate under rainbows, forgetful of
us beneath great girders of the grey clouds –
Where did you ponder the gospels of that strict
navigation? –

Night travellers joyful among jewelled harness of
darkness,
Hurling yourselves at hot suns risen smoking
before you,
Or burying brilliance in the panes of their waters,
and you
Exultant between emptiness blue above and blue
below you.

Mist and darkness begin now to gather and the
small rain falls heavily –
And here with the sad, with the finished, fleeting
enchanters, you leave me,
With the rain, and the ruffian wind rising, and
these shabby old men standing bowed all
about me –
Who are these grey mutterers? – ach, hateful,
rancid,
With thick glasses and ear-plugs, white hairs and
holes in their trousers –
Oh, birds, darling thieves and bewitchers, at your
going we are weary, sad,
We are sick and defeated, all are abandoned, with
tears on our cheeks
And with great weights heavy on our hearts.

Jordan

I am worried. Today when I cut my chin with my white-handled razor I didn't bleed. That was the way Danny's shaving went. Danny was my friend. Together we had a spell working the fairs and markets out there in that country where there are nothing but farms and chapels. It was a sort of uncivilized place. I had invented a good line, a special cube guaranteed to keep the flies off the meat, and Danny had his little round boxes of toothpaste. This toothpaste he scraped off a big lump of wet batter, a few pounds of it, greenish in colour and with a bad smell; it stood on a tin plate and sometimes Danny would sell it as corn cure. So as to gather a crowd around his trestle he used to strip down to his black tights and walk about with a fifty-six-pound solid iron weight hanging by a short strap from his teeth. This was to show what wonderful teeth you would have if you used Danny's toothpaste. It was only when he was doing this that you ever saw any colour in Danny's face. The colour came because he did the walking about upside down; he was on his hands doing it with his black stockings in the air.

Danny was thin and undersized. If I made a joke about his skinny legs he would lower his lids offended and say, 'Don't be so personal.' He was very touchy. His tights were coms dyed black and they looked half empty, as though large slices had been cut off from inside them. He had a fine, half-starved face, very thin and leathery, like a sad cow. There was only one thing wrong with his face and that was the ears. Danny's ears were big and yellow, and they stood out at right angles to his head. From the front they looked as though they had been screwed into his skull, and one had been screwed in a lot further than the other. His straight carrot hair was very long and thick and brushed back over his head. When he scuffled about on his bandy arms with that half hundredweight dangling from his teeth, his mop opened downwards off his scalp as though it was on a hinge, and bumped along the cobble-stones. He was very proud of his teeth. He thought so much of them he never showed them to anyone. Nobody ever saw Danny grinning.

My own line was that special cube I had invented to keep the flies off the meat. I used to soften down a few candles and shape the grease into dices with my fingers. Then I put one or two of these white dices on a cut of meat on my trestle in the middle of the market crowds. There were always plenty of fat flies and bluebottles buzzing about in those markets, what with the boiled sweet stalls and the horse-droppings, but you never saw one perching on my meat with the white cubes on it. This wasn't because the flies didn't like candle-grease but because under the meat-plate I had a saucer of paraffin oil.

One night Danny and I were sitting on the bed in our lodging house. The place was filthy and lousy and we were catching bugs on our needles off the walls and roasting them to death one by one in the candle flame. Danny was bitter. The fair had finished but the farmers had kept their hands on their ha'pennies. And the weather was bad, very wet and gusty and cold all the time. Danny said we were pioneers. He said these farmers were savages, they didn't care about having filthy teeth, or eating their food fly-blown. He was very down-hearted. He hadn't had much to eat for a few days and between the noisy bursting of the bugs his empty belly crowed. I was down-hearted too. We had to get money from somewhere to pay for our lodgings and a seat in the horsebrake drawing out of town the next morning. I asked Danny to come out into the town to see what we could pick up but he wouldn't. At first he said it was too cold. Then he said he had got to darn his tights and his stockings. In the end I went by myself.

The town had been newly wetted with another downpour and Danny was right about the cold. As I walked up the dark empty main street I could feel the wind blowing into the holes in my boots. Everywhere was closed up and silent and deserted. I looked in at 'The Bell' and 'The Feathers' and 'The

Glyndŵr', but they were all empty. Then from the swing door of 'The Black Horse' I saw inside a big broad-shouldered man sitting down by himself in the bar. Apart from him the bar was deserted. He was by the fire and his back was towards me. I knew bumming a drink out of him would be as easy as putting one hand in the other. I knew this because he had a red wig on coming down over the collar of his coat, and a man who wears a wig is lonely.

On the table in front of the man I could see a glass of whisky and in his hand was a little black book. He was singing a hymn out of it in Welsh. It was sad, a funeral hymn, but very determined. I stood by the door of the empty bar and listened. The 'Horse' was small and gloomy inside. I wondered if I would go in. The man seemed huge in the neck and across the shoulders, and every time he moved all the flesh on him seemed to begin to tremble. If he kept dead still he stopped trembling. I went in past him and stood the other side of the table by the fire.

When I got round to the front of this man something snapped like a carrot inside me. His face was hideous. The flesh of it looked as though it had been torn apart into ribbons and shoved together again anyhow back on to the bones. Long white scars ran glistening through the purple skin like ridges of gristle. Only his nose had escaped. This was huge and dark and full of holes, it curved out like a big black lump of wood with the worm in it. He was swarthy, as though he was sitting in a bar of shadow, and I looked up to see if perhaps a roof-beam had come between him and the hanging oil-lamp lighting the bar. There wasn't a hair on him, no moustache or eyebrows, but his wig was like the bright feathers of a red hen. It started a long way back, half way up his scalp, and the gristly scars streamed down over his forehead and cheekbones from under it. He had a tidy black suit on and a good thick-soled boot with grease rubbed in. The other leg was what looked like a massive iron pipe blocked up at the end with a solid wooden plug. It came out on to the hearth from the turn-up of his trousers.

It is best to tell the tale when you haven't got any cash to put on the counter. When I began to talk to him by the fire, I tucked my feet under the settle and said I was a salesman. Although Danny and I could put all our belongings in a tobacco-box, I soon had a fine range of second-hand goods for sale. The man closed his little book to listen. He told me he was Jordan, man-servant to the old doctor of the town. I took a polished piece of rabbit's backbone out of my waistcoast pocket and passed it over to him. It looked like a small cow's skull, complete with horns. He examined it slowly, trembling all the time. He had huge soft hands and his finger-nails were as green as grass. I told him he could keep it. He called for whisky for both of us.

As I drank my whisky I enjoyed thinking what I had for sale, I had a little harmonium, portable, very good for Welsh hymns, perfect except for a rip in the bellows; a new invention that would get a cork out of a bottle – like that!; a nice line in leather purses, a free gift presented with each one – a brass watch-key, number eight, or a row of glass-headed pins; a pair of solid leather knee-boots, just the thing for him because they were both for the same leg. The man's eyes were small, they looked half closed up, and he watched me hard without moving them all the time. In the heat of the fire a strong smell came off him. It was a damp clinging smell, clammy, like the mildewed corner of some old church, up there behind the organ where they keep the bier. At last he bent forward and held his smashed face close to mine. I stopped talking. He trembled and said softly, 'I am interested in buying only one thing.'

Somehow I felt mesmerized, I couldn't say anything. I am not often like that. I lifted my eyebrows.

Jordan didn't answer. His little eyes slid round the empty bar. Then he moved his lips into a word that staggered me. I stared at him. For a minute by the blazing bar fire I went cold as clay. He nodded his head and made the same mouthing of his smashed face as before. The word he shaped out was, 'Corpses'.

There was dead silence between us. The clock in the bar echoed loudly, like a long-legged horse trotting down an empty street. But I let my face go into a twist and I squeezed a tear into the end of my eye. I crossed myself and offered the serving man the body of my brother. I had buried him, I remembered, a week ago come tomorrow.

Jordan took his hat and stick out of the corner. The stick was heavy, with a lot of rope wound round it, and the black hat had a wide brim. When he stood up he was like a giant rising above me. He was much bigger even than I thought. He looked down hard at the little bone I had given him and then threw it on the back of the fire. We went out into the street. As we walked along, his iron leg bumped on the pavement and made a click-clicking noise like a carried bucket. He would show me where to bring the corpse and I was to come between midnight and daybreak.

We walked together out of the town into the country. It was pitch dark and soon the way was through wet fields. It was still cold but I didn't feel it any more. Jordan had this peg leg but he was big, and I sweated keeping up with him. He trembled all the time as he walked but his shaking didn't make you think he was weak. He was like a powerful machine going full force and making the whole throbbing engine-house tremble to the foundations with its power. I trotted behind him breathless. He was so busy singing the Welsh burial hymn that he didn't drop a word to me all the way.

At last we came to a gate across the lane we were following. There was a farm-house beyond it, all in darkness. Jordan stopped singing and shouted, twice. There was no reply. He started singing again. He poised himself on his iron leg and his walking stick and gave the gate a great kick with his good foot. It fell flat. We found ourselves going at full speed across a farmyard. A heavy sheepdog ran out of the shadows barking and showing a fringe of teeth. He looked huge and fierce enough to tear us in pieces. Jordan didn't pause and I kept close behind him. The dog changed his gallop into a stiff-legged prowl, and he filled his throat with a terrible snarl. Then suddenly he sprang straight at Jordan's throat. As he rose in the air Jordan hit him a ringing crack on the head with his stick. He used both hands to bring it down. The dog dropped to the pebbles of the yard passing a contented sigh. He didn't move again. Jordan put his good foot on him and brought the stick down on his head again and again. He went on doing this, his sad hymn getting louder and louder, until the dog's brains came out. I went cold in my sweat to hear him. At last he wiped the handle of the stick in the grass of the hedge and went on down the lane, singing.

We came in sight of the lights of a big house. 'That's the place,' he said. 'Bring it round to the back door. Good night.'

He went off into the darkness like a giant in his broad-brimmed hat. I wiped the sweat off my head. After he had disappeared I could hear his hymn and his leg clicking for a long time. His hymn was slow and sad, but it didn't make me unhappy at all. It frightened the life out of me.

On the way back to the town I kicked the dead dog into the ditch.

Danny never let his job slide off his back. As I climbed up the stairs of our lodging house I came face to face with two eyes watching me through the upright bars of the top-landing banister. It was Danny dawdling about on his hands, practising. I had a lot of trouble persuading him to be a corpse. All he had to do was pretend to be dead and to let me and the blackman on the landing below carry him out to the doctor's house. Then when we were paid and everybody in the house was asleep he could get out of one of the downstairs windows. We would be waiting for him. We could leave the town by the first brake in the morning. It was safe as houses. Nothing could go wrong. At last Danny agreed.

At midnight the three of us set out for Jordan's

house. We were me, Danny and Marky. Marky was a half-caste cheapjack, a long thin shiny man the colour of gunmetal, selling fire-damaged remnants and bankrupt stock and that. He used to dribble and paw you at close quarters but he would do anything you asked him for tuppence or thruppence. We walked through the fields carrying a rolled-up sack and my trestle until we came in sight of the house Jordan had shown me. Danny stripped to his coms under a tree and hid his clothes. He put on an old cream-flannel nightgown Marky had brought out of stock. Then we sewed him in the sack and put him on the planks of my trestle. It was pitch dark and cold, with the small rain drizzling down again as fine as pepper.

The doctor's house was all in darkness. We went round to the little pointed wooden door at the back of the garden. I whispered to Danny to ask if he was all right. There were two answers, Danny's teeth chattering and the uproar of dogs howling and barking inside the garden. I had never thought about dogs. What were we going to do?

At once I heard the click of the leg the other side of the wall and Jordan's voice speaking. 'Down, Farw. Down, Angau,' he growled. The narrow pointed door was thrown open, and suddenly we saw Jordan. He was stripped naked to the half and he had left off his wig. He looked so huge, so powerful and ugly in the doorway, with his swelling nose and his fleshy body all slashed, I almost let go of our load with fright. And behind him the hounds, three of them, black and shaggy and big as ponies, yelped and bayed and struggled to get past him to attack us. Jordan spoke sharply to them and at last we were able to carry Danny into the garden. He was as light on the boards as a bag of hay. Jordan spoke only to the dogs. He made a sign and led us hobbling along the pebble path across the yard towards some dark out-houses. The three hounds paced whining beside us, sniffing all the time at the sack and spilling their dribble.

The room we went into smelt like a stable. It was dim and empty but there was an oil lamp hanging from a nail in a low beam. We laid Danny across some feed-boxes under this lamp. Jordan stood back by the stable door with the whimpering dogs while we were doing it, watching us all the time. I could feel his eyes burning into my back. His skin was very dark and his chest bulged up into big paps resting above his powerful folded arms. But all his body was torn with terrible wounds like his face. Long shining scars like the glistening veins you see running through the rocks of a cliff-face spread in all directions over his flesh. His bald head had a large dome on it and that was covered with scars too. His whole body gleamed down to his waist, the drizzle had given him a high shine like the gloos of varnish.

We left Danny lying on the boards across the feed-boxes and came back up to the door to ask for our money. Jordan didn't reply. Instead he took a large clasp-knife out of the pocket in the front of his trousers and opened it. Then, ordering the dogs to stay, he went past us and bumped over to where Danny was lying in his sack. He seemed to take a long time to get there. There was dead silence. As he went from us we could see a black hole in his back you could put your fist into. My skin prickled. Marky's eyes rolled with the dogs sniffing him and he began to paw the air. I looked round and saw a hay-fork with a stumpy leg in the corner. Jordan turned round under the lamp and looked back at us. The blade of the open knife trembled in his hand. He turned again and cut open the sewing in the sack above Danny's face. I could hardly breathe. Danny was so white under the hanging lamp I thought he was really dead. My hair stirred. Danny's teeth showed shining in his open mouth, and in the lamplight falling right down upon them the whites of his half-opened eyes glistened. He was pale and stiff, as if he had already begun to rot. Jordan bent over, gazing down at him with the knife in his hand, the lamp spreading a shine over the skin of his wet back. I was frightened, but if Danny's teeth chattered or his belly crowed I was willing to use that pitchfork to get us out. At last Jordan turned. He spoke for the first time.

'He is a good corpse,' he said.

'He is my brother,' I told him.

'Where did you get him from?'

'I dug him up.'

He nodded. He left the knife open on the feed-box and came over to us. Putting his hand again into his front pocket he brought out a large lump of wadding. This he opened and in the middle lay three gold sovereigns. He passed the coins over to me with his huge trembling hands and motioned us out roughly. He went back and blew out the oil lamp and we left Danny alone there in the darkness. Jordan locked the stable door and the hounds trotted round us growling as we left the garden through the little door.

'Good night,' said Jordan.

'Good night, brother,' I said.

We walked about in the fields, trying to keep warm, waiting for the time to go back to get Danny out. Marky had gone icy cold. I was worried, especially about those dogs. I wished I had a drop of drink inside me. When we thought everything would be quiet again we went back to see if it was safe to give Danny the whistle. I threw my coat over the bottle-glass stuck on top of the garden wall and climbed up. I could see a candle lit in a downstairs window of the doctor's house and by its light Jordan moved about inside the room in his nightshirt and nightcap. Presently his light disappeared and all was in darkness.

An owl in a tree close by started screeching. Marky was frightened and climbed up on to the garden wall to be near me. There was no sign of Jordan's dogs in the garden. It was bitterly cold up there on top of the wall without our coats on. The wind was lazy, it went right through us instead of going round. It had stopped raining again. There was a moon now but it was small and a long way off, very high up in the sky, and shrunken enough to go into your cap.

We waited a long time shivering and afraid to talk. Marky's eyes were like glass marbles. At last I saw something moving in the shadows by the stable. My heart shot up hot into my throat. Marky caught hold of me trembling like a leaf. A figure in white began to creep along the wall. It was Danny. He must have got out through one of the stable windows. I whistled softly to him and at that there was uproar. The three hounds came bounding across the yard from nowhere, making straight for Danny, baying and snarling like mad. I didn't know what to do for the moment with fright. The dogs were almost on top of him. Danny sprang on to his hands and began trotting towards them. His black legs waved in the air and his night-shirt fell forward and hung down to the ground over his head. The dogs stopped dead when they saw him. Then they turned together and galloped away into the shadows howling with fright. When Danny reached the wall we grabbed him firmly by the ankles and pulled him up out of the garden at one pluck. We were not long getting back to our lodging-house. The next morning we paid our landlord and the brake driver with one of the sovereigns we had had off Jordan.

I didn't have any luck. All the rest of the summer it was still wet and there were hardly any flies. I tried selling elephant charms, very lucky, guaranteed, but the harvest failed and in the end I couldn't even give them away. Danny got thinner and thinner and more quiet. He was like a rush. He had nothing to say. There never was much in his head except the roots of his hair. Having been a corpse was on his mind. And he was like a real corpse to sleep with, as cold as ice and all bones. He lost interest even in standing on his hands.

We visited a lot of the towns that held fairs but without much luck. One market day we were sitting in a coffee tavern. It was a ramshackle place built of wooden planks put up for the market day in a field behind the main street. The floor was only grass and the tables and benches stood on it. You could get a plate of peas and a cup of tea there cheap. Danny didn't care about food now even when we had it. Because it was market day this coffee tavern was crowded. It was very close inside, enough to make you faint, and the wasps were buzzing everywhere. All the people around us were jabbering Welsh and eating food out of newspapers.

Presently, above the noise, I heard a bumping and clicking sound in the passage. I felt as though a bath-full of icy water had shot over me inside my clothes. I looked round but there was no way of escape. Then I heard the funeral hymn. In a minute Jordan was standing in the entrance of the coffee tavern. He was huge, bigger than ever, a doorful. In one hand was his roped-up stick and in the other his black hymn-book. His broad-brimmed hat was on his head, but instead of his wig he had a yellow silk handkerchief under it with the corners knotted. He stopped singing and stood in the doorway looking round for an empty seat. A man from our table just then finished his peas and went out. Jordan saw the empty place and hobbled in. We couldn't escape him. He came clicking through the eating crowd like an earthquake and sat down at our table opposite us.

At first I didn't know what to do. Danny had never seen Jordan and was staring down at the grease floating on his tea. I tried to go on leading the peas up to my mouth on my spoon but I could hardly do it. Jordan was opposite, watching me. He could see I was shaking. I pretended to fight the wasps. I could feel his bright bunged-up eyes on me all the time. He put his arms in a ring on the table and leaned over towards me. I was spilling the peas in my fright. I couldn't go on any longer. I lowered my spoon and looked at him. He was so hideous at close quarters I almost threw up. The big black block of his nose reached out at me, full of worm-holes, and the rest of his face looked as though it had been dragged open with hooks. But he was smiling.

'Jordan,' I said, although my tongue was like a lump of cork. 'Mr Jordan.'

He nodded. 'You've come back,' he said. 'Where have you been keeping?'

The whole coffee tavern seemed to be trembling with his movements. I felt as though I was in the stifling loft of some huge pipe-organ, with the din coming out full blast and all the hot woodwork in a shudder. His question had me stammering. I told him I had been busy. My business kept me moving, I travelled about a lot. The wooden building around me felt suffocating, airless as a glasshouse. I glanced at Danny. He looked as though he had been tapped and all his blood run off. Even his yellow ears had turned chalky.

Jordan nodded again, grinning his terrible grin. 'The chick born in hell returns to the burning,' he said. All the time he watched me from under the front knot of his yellow handkerchief. He ignored Danny altogether. His eyes were small, but they looked as though each one had had a good polish before being put into his head.

'Our bargain was a good one,' he went on, still smiling. 'Very good. It turned out well.'

I was afraid he would hear my swallow at work, it sounded loud even above the jabbering. 'I am glad,' I said, 'I did my best. I always do my best.'

'My master was pleased,' he said. He leaned forward and beckoned me towards him. I bent my head to listen and his wooden nose was up touching my ear. 'A splendid corpse,' he whispered. 'Inside, a mass of corruption. Tumours and malignant growths. Exactly what my master needed. Cut up beautifully, it did.'

There was a loud sigh from Danny. When I turned to look at him he wasn't there. He had gone down off his bench in a heap on the grass. People all round got up from their tables and crowded round. Some of them waved their arms and shouted. 'Give him air,' they said, 'he's fainted. Give him air.' For a minute I forgot all about Jordan. I told the people Danny was my friend. They carried him out of the coffee tavern and laid him on the grass at the side of the road. 'Loosen his neck,' somebody said, and his rubber breast and collar were snatched off showing his black coms underneath. The crowd came on like flies round jam. At last Danny opened his eyes. Someone brought him a glass of water out of the coffee tavern. He sat up, bowed his shoulders and put his hands over his face as though he was crying. I spotted something then I had never noticed before. There was a big bald hole in his red hair at the top of his head. He looked sickly. But before long he could stand again. I pushed his breast and collar into my pocket and took him back to our lodging house. I looked round but I couldn't see Jordan at all in the crowd. Danny was in bed for a week. He was never the same again. For one thing if he cut himself shaving he didn't bleed. The only thing that came out of the cut was a kind of yellow water.

Before the year was out I had buried Danny. It was wild weather and he caught a cold standing about half-naked in his tights in the fairs and markets. He took to his bed in our lodgings. Soon he was light-headed and then unconscious. Every night I sat by him in our bedroom under the roof with the candle lit, listening to his breathing.

One night I dropped off to sleep in the chair and he woke me up screaming. He dreamt Jordan was trying to chop his hands off to make him walk on the stumps. I was terrified at the noise he made. The candle went out and the roar of the wind sawing at the roof of the house was deafening. My heart was thumping like a drum as I tried to relight the candle. I couldn't stop Danny screaming. A few minutes later he died with a yell. Poor Danny.

Being a corpse was too much for him. He never struggled out from under the paws of his memories.

The next night the man from the parish came. He asked me if I wasn't ashamed to bury my friend like that. He meant that Danny hadn't had a shave for a week. In the candle-light he had a bright copper beard and he wasn't quite so much like a cow. When the man had gone I started to shave the corpse. It was hard doing it by candle light. High up on the cheek-bone I must have done something wrong, I must have cut him, because he opened one of his eyes and looked hard at me with it. I was more careful after that. I didn't want to open that vein they say is full of lice.

The morning of the funeral I borrowed a black tie off our landlord. I bummed a wreath on strap. It was very pretty. It was a lot of white flowers on wires made into the shape of a little armchair. In the bars of the back was a card with the word 'Rest' on it done in forget-me-nots. Danny always liked something religious like that.

There was nobody in the funeral except the parson and me and two gravediggers. It was a bad day in autumn and very stormy. The long grass in the graveyard was lying down smooth under the flow of the wind. There were some willow trees around the wall all blown bare except for a few leaves sticking to the thin twigs like hair-nits. The parson in his robes was a thin man but he looked fat in the wind. As he gabbled the service, the big dried-up leaves blown along the path scratched at the gravel with webbed fingers, like cut-off hands. I wanted to run away. When Danny was in the earth, the gravediggers left. The parson and I sang a funeral hymn. The wind was roaring. As we were singing I heard another voice joining in in the distance. It was faint. I had been waiting for it. I didn't need to look round. I knew the sound of the voice was deafening, the sad hymn roaring like a waterfall beside me. Jordan came right up and stood between me and the parson, touching me. For shaking he was like a giant tree hurling off the storm. His little black book was in his hand. Even in the wind I could smell the strong mouldiness that came off him, clammy as grave-clay. He was bigger than ever. The brim of his black hat was spread out like a roof over my head. As he stood beside me he seemed to be absorbing me. He put his arm with the night-stick in his hand around my shoulders. I felt as though I was gradually disappearing inside his huge body. The ground all around me melted, the path began to flow faster and faster past my feet like a rushing river. I tried to shout out in my terror. I fainted.

When I came round the parson was beside me. We were sitting on the heap of earth beside Danny's open grave. I was as wet as the bed of the river with fright. When I spoke to the parson about Jordan he humoured me. That was a fortnight ago. Yesterday when I cut myself shaving I didn't bleed. All that came out of the cut was a drop or two of yellow water. I won't be long now. I am finished. I wouldn't advise anybody to try crossing Jordan.

For further reading

Poetry

Poems (The Fortune Press, 1939)
The Dream of Jake Hopkins (The Fortune Press, 1954)
Selected Poems (Gomer Press, 1975)
Selected Poems: Fragments and Fictions (Poetry Wales Press, 1988)
A People's Poetry (Seren, 1997)
Collected Poems, ed. Meic Stephens (University of Wales Press, 1996)

Poetry and prose

Goodbye, What Were You? (Gomer, 1994)

Prose

The Blue Bed (Jonathan Cape, 1937)
The Water Music (George Routledge & Sons, 1944)
The Valley, The City, The Village (J.M. Dent, 1956)
The Learning Lark (J.M. Dent, 1960)
The Island of Apples (J.M. Dent, 1965; ed. Belinda Humfrey, University of Wales Press, 1992)
Selected Short Stories (J.M. Dent, 1971)
Welsh Heirs (Gomer Press, 1977)
Collected Stories, ed. Tony Brown (University of Wales Press, 1999)

Autobiography

The Dragon Has Two Tongues (J.M. Dent, 1968; ed. Tony Brown, University of Wales Press, 2001)

Criticism

Leslie Norris, *Glyn Jones*, in the *Writers of Wales* series (University of Wales Press, 1973; reprinted 1997)

Images of Wales

The Corgi Series covers, no.21
'Walking in Blaen-cwm', Charles Burton

Charles Burton
Charles Burton is one of our great artists. By his early twenties his work was being swept up by public institutions and important private collectors, and he won the Gold Medal for Fine Art at the National Eisteddfod when he was only 25. But he has always been a very private painter. Like many of the artists we value most (Blake, Cézanne and Gwen John spring to mind), he has painted not for an audience, for dealers or curators, but for himself. Painting has been his life, and at no time in the past fifty years has he stopped exploring and enquiring. Yet by his own choice there have been long gaps between appearances in public; enough for us to need to be reminded of his stature. Recently, his work has once again been shown and critically acclaimed, and has appeared in books, magazines and television programmes.

He was born in Treherbert in 1929, and grew up enveloped in the warm embrace of the Rhondda Fawr between the wars. Many of his paintings then, and now, are about his love for this extraordinary place. At Cardiff College of Art in the late 1940s he was at the heart of the Rhondda

Group, alongside his friends Ernie Zobole and Glyn Morgan. They painted their responses to their everyday surroundings with individuality and freshness, and together had a powerful influence on contemporary Welsh art. After post-graduate studies at the Royal College he became a teacher known for his ability to see talent and develop it. He was Head of Painting at Liverpool College of Art (where one failing student for whom he won another chance was John Lennon), and from 1970 to his retirement, Head of Art and Design at the Polytechnic of Wales.

Charles Burton has absorbed lessons from artists of every age and idiom, and channelled them to his own vision. Like a conjurer he takes pleasure in the elegant solution of a paradox or problem. Look at the complex challenges he sets himself in composition, but see how, after weeks or sometimes months of struggle, he resolves them with apparent ease, and wins the quality he admires most, simplicity. He has embraced many subjects: landscapes, still-lifes, interiors, figures, but his works are unified in painterly balance of pictorial space and in the love that they express. They need a kind of reverie to be absorbed. So quietly perfect are they that they may be lost to those who hurry for an instant impact. But look hard and long, and they will never lose their value.

Peter Wakelin

DEATH TRAPP

The only person now in danger from Ulrike's bomb was the bomb disposal expert. His helmeted head bent above the boot of the car. Cautiously he turned the handle and lifted. He moved very slowly and very gently. Inside he saw the bomb, the wires trailing in a more amateur fashion than he would have expected from the reputation of this little lot. The timing device tick-tocked away. He looked . . .

Also by Ken Blake in Sphere Books:

THE PROFESSIONALS 1: WHERE THE JUNGLE ENDS
THE PROFESSIONALS 2: LONG SHOT
THE PROFESSIONALS 3: STAKE OUT
THE PROFESSIONALS 4: HUNTER HUNTED
THE PROFESSIONALS 5: BLIND RUN
THE PROFESSIONALS 6: FALL GIRL
THE PROFESSIONALS 7: HIDING TO NOTHING
THE PROFESSIONALS 8: DEAD RECKONING
THE PROFESSIONALS 10: CRY WOLF

THE PROFESSIONALS:

No Stone

KEN BLAKE

Based on the original screenplays by
Tony Barwick and Roger Marshall

SPHERE BOOKS LIMITED
30/32 Gray's Inn Road, London WC1X 8JL

First published by Sphere Books Ltd 1981

TRADE
MARK

Set in Baskerville

Printed and bound in England by
Cox & Wyman, Reading

Chapter One

A single star splintered from the edge of the blade as Quinn brought the axe down. With controlled power Quinn's blow split the log with a single clean sweep of the axe. The two half logs, their newly-exposed yellow interiors bright and shining, quivered, toppled, fell. Quinn reached for another log.

The sounds of axe splitting wood and the dry tumble of the cleft logs barely disturbed the peace of Repton Clinic. Safe, secure, discreet behind its high wall and iron gates, Repton cared for men like Quinn, men who were no longer fully in contact with reality.

A large, strongly built man, Quinn, in the prime of life, tough and fit. He wore a white sweat shirt and pants that were baggy from exercise, his trainers were scuffed.

He took the next log up, lifting it easily one-handed, positioned it on the chopping block.

His face expressed only a blank concern over what he was doing right here and now. One of Repton's male nurses walked towards the brick yard where the wood was chopped. A strong, professional man, he shared enough concern for the patients here to make the life bearable. He put a hand on Quinn's shoulder.

Quinn stopped moving. Like a forest creature abruptly scenting a predator, he remained stone-still, unmoving, wary, and yet, somehow, lifeless.

'You're wanted, Quinn. Doctor Grey.'

As though a machine activated to obey a command, Quinn lowered his axe. The male nurse took it away, placed it beside the chopping block. He began to lead Quinn away.

Quinn hesitated.

Worried, his gaze fastened on the untidy pile of logs he'd chopped and which he had not yet stacked. Stacking logs was just as much a part of the job as chopping them . . .

The male nurse urged him along, gently.

'It's all right ...'

Obeying the new command, Quinn allowed himself to be led off.

The early sun had brought out the flowers, and a glisten on the grass lent it that golden-yellow sheen. The trees fringing the extensive grounds looked dark green and sober by contrast. Quinn walked along with his head hanging, looking where he was going, and that was all.

Repton's original buildings dated way back, all turrets and gothic arches and crumbling stonework; there were new buildings jutting out at the back, but these were discreetly hidden by newly-planted stands of trees. They parked the cars back there, too. The male nurse led Quinn past the deeply mullioned windows of the old building to the side entrance.

They passed a flower bed and the male nurse sniffed appreciatively, always did like a spot of gardening when he got the chance. Quinn just walked on in that plodding way without lifting his head, without noticing the glorious scent of the flowers. They went up the short flight of steps and in through the brown-painted doorway.

Doctor Grey's surgery was just off to the right and the male nurse noticed the waiting room door was wide open. He ushered Quinn through, and called: 'Doctor Grey.'

There was no answer but the male nurse wasn't surprised. Doctor Grey had a busy schedule, and this business with Quinn was purely routine. He pointed to a chair.

'Sit down, Quinn. The doctor will be right with you.'

Obediently, Quinn sat down in the chair. The male nurse gave him a calculating look and went out knowing that Quinn was a vegetable, anyway and perfectly safe. That job done he could look forward to a quick cuppa before getting on with the next. It was all go at Repton.

He left the door to the waiting room open as he went. There was no one in there, apart from Quinn sitting in the surgery waiting for Doctor Grey, and the place was very quiet.

Quinn did not bother to look up when the doctor entered. He was willing to accept what went on, finding things difficult to grasp, accepting what these people did. A chink of surgical instruments from the enamel trays on a side table did make his eyes flick in that direction. But that was merely the involuntary reaction of reflexes, once honed, still retaining some of their old quickness.

From the tray the doctor lifted a hypodermic needle.

'Hold up your arm.'

The patient's reaction was slow. His face expressed the dawning of a wince, a vague suggestion of withdrawal, even of refusal. But, obediently, he held out his arm. The hand was broad and firm, the nails trimmed and square cut. Muscles ridged on the bare arm, hairs glistening.

The doctor swabbed the antiseptic with precise movements. He poised the prepared needle. It stabbed down.

As the needle pricked Quinn's bare arm, he looked up into the doctor's face for the first time.

The doctor's face looked down with calm detachment, a professional doing his job. He was in his mid thirties, fair-haired, with the look to his face that told you he was strong-minded. His white coat was freshly startched.

Quinn shivered.

Abruptly, Quinn tried to stand up. Sweat started out on his forehead. The doctor held onto him. Both men said not a word; this struggle was beyond the need for words, was the primitive instinct of hunting and survival. The doctor kept up his pressure, forcing the needle home against Quinn's galvanic struggles to break free.

With a ferocious lunge Quinn struggled away. The doctor half-fell, half-stood back as the big man roared to his feet. The tray of instruments went flying with a clatter lost in Quinn's bull roar.

Sheened in sweat, his eyes wild, shaking, Quinn wrenched around. He ran like a madman across the surgery, flung an arm across his face, and dived headfirst through the window.

His broad shoulders took the wood and glass with him in a splintering shower. Shrapnel splashes of glitter in the sunshine, the glass scattered across the gravel. Quinn was up and running in an instant.

Two male nurses strolling around the corner to fetch

patients heard the shattering smash of the window's destruction. They saw Quinn bursting away across the lawns. They shouted.

'Hey, you! Stop! Stop!'

With the habitual obedience that had been his companion for so many years, Quinn halted. He swung about. He panted, his head was thrust forward, his jaw hard. He glared at the oncoming male nurses in their white coats.

The nurses ran towards him.

Quinn saw them – he saw the two men quite clearly. They wore grey-green uniforms, with red tabs. Their hats were hard and round. They had cradled Kalashnikovs at their sides. They were K.G.B. guards, and their shouts to him to stop were in Russian.

The male nurses reached Quinn.

His eyes were wide open, fixed, staring. Sweat poured from him. He uttered a desperate mewling sound.

As the nurses reached for him, he broke away, sent them staggering. As they fell Quinn turned and ran with maniacal strength away from the clinic, across the lawns, heading for the main gateway.

He breathed in a hoarse gasping, ragged with effort; yet the effort did not come from running. He was in perfect physical condition and could have run miles. The whole world was going up and down beyond his vision. He could see the iron gates and the gateposts, and the men standing there.

He saw the gatemen quite clearly. They saw a patient in a white sweat shirt and slacks running towards them in the most terrible state, and braced themselves.

Quinn saw them . . .

He saw the heavily guarded gateway, the frowning machine-gun slits in the upper parapet, the barbed wire. He saw the guards in their grey-green. He stopped in his tracks, panting for breath, now, panting like a hunted animal. The gateway was the guarded frontier post, and now one of the guards lifted his Kalashnikov. The rifle centred on Quinn.

He broke and ran, weaving from side to side, and in his ears the staccato crack of rifle shots blasted wings into flight. He ran, bursting for breath, crashed past the end of the angle of wall, ploughed across rose beds.

Ironically, the roses were Peace.

He staggered on and felt the tug at his trousers.

He looked down.

He saw quite clearly the viciously snarling dog tearing at his leg. The dog swung his head from side to side, savaging him. Quinn wrenched himself free with a supreme effort, gulping air, and ran on, blindly, running, running.

The male nurses pursuing him followed across the rose beds, catching their trousers, as Quinn had done, on the rose thorns. Quinn reached the wall. For only a moment he stood against the wall, panting, looking up, gauging the jump.

The sounds of his pursuers menaced him, mingled with the ferocious baying of the dogs. They sounded very close. He could hear the fluent Russian words of command, to seize him and drag him back – he leaped.

He got a hand onto the top of the wall and gripped.

He started to pull himself up and felt a touch on his leg.

One of the male nurses, quicker than the others, reached the wall and made a grab for Quinn's leg.

Quinn looked down.

He saw the guard quite clearly. He saw the uniform and the sub-machine gun, he saw the flat, round hat, he saw the leering face as the man reached out to grab him and haul him off the wall.

With his free foot, Quinn lashed out, a savage and brutal kick.

The man yelled and fell away, holding his face.

Quinn chinned himself desperately, wriggled around on top of the wall, dropped out of sight.

The bunch of male nurses, puffing, halted and then started to run towards the gate. They were too late.

A man named Quinn was free.

Sitting astride his bike at the corner of Angel Street and watching the traffic flow past in an orderly fashion along Gainsforth Road, Bill Eversely wished he was off duty already. He had a big night planned with Gloria tonight – the works. The sun on his helmet didn't bother him, and the big bike was a comforting bulk beneath. Being a motorbike policeman had perks and disasters; but Bill Eversely knew what he liked to do.

The traffic flow was momentarily interrupted.

A white Capri fleeted past so quickly Eversely thought for a whole three heartbeats he was seeing a ghost car.

Then he forgot all about Gloria and his plans for tonight.

'The cheeky blighter!' he said to himself and jumped on the old kickstarter. The big bike roared, the glasses came down, the throttle was given the old twist and away shot Bill Eversely on the tail of a road hog.

The bike weaved in and out of traffic and then belted along a straight ... Passing cars fleeted past in a blur.

The white Capri speeded up ahead.

In the passenger seat Ray Doyle looked back through the rear window. His round cheerful face expressed profound sorrow. He slumped forward again.

'Want to stop?'

Bodie lifted his right foot.

'We're late already. Couple of minutes won't make any difference.'

His sleek appearance was quite noticeable, even against the new image that Ray Doyle had achieved. Both men wore smart suits, looking immaculate. Both men knew that fashion-plate smartness could be frazzled into muddied and torn wreckage any minute in their line of business.

Bodie hit the brake hard.

The Capri slewed into a shuddering halt by the kerb.

Bill Eversely hit his own brake and just had time to slide into the kerb astern of the Capri. He breathed in hard. Stiff legged, he got off his bike and propped it.

He strolled towards the Capri with just the hint of a swagger, just a faint touch of the old West gunfighter stalking down the main street, Peacemaker on hip ... As he walked, so he slowly drew off his right gauntlet.

Bodie wound down his window.

The patrolman leaned in.

'Good morning, funny man. I made it sixty-five.' Eversely slapped his gauntlet against his leg. 'But then, I'm not vindictive. I'm going to call it sixty-five.'

Bodie said: 'Well, we could say we were on our way to a fire.'

Bill Eversely let that pass him by without turning a hair. 'Driving licence.'

Bodie reached under his coat and pulled out his CI5 identification, handed it through the open window. Eversely took it, flipped it open, felt the muscles in his face tauten.

'What's this?'

'CI5.'

'Huh.' Bill Eversely knew as much as anyone about CI5, the Big A, the squad that did not hit the headlines but whose antics caused many a villain nightmares. He knew the name. He knew the clout the name carried. Apart from that – he knew damn all. 'Thunder and lightning brigade,' he said, with a flash of spirit that surprised himself. 'You *are* on official business?'

He handed the ID card back.

Doyle said, casually: 'Course we are.'

Bodie nodded and without winding up the window gunned the Capri away.

Bill Eversely looked after the car. He frowned. Those thud and blunder boys could just as easily be going to the launderette. He was a motorcycle cop. He wondered if he'd care to join the Big A. You did hear some funny stories, and for all the little he really knew about the department, some of those stories had the whiff of truth. Criminal Intelligence Five had been set up by warrant of the Home Office and umpteen high brass departments to fight crime and use unorthodox methods, methods criminals used themselves in this modern scientific world. He walked back to his bike.

At least, he understood bikes, and he knew what he wanted to do tonight with Gloria.

He wondered, as he stamped on the starter, what those two high-powered lads would be doing tonight . . .

Those two agents of the Big A saw the man waiting for them in the railed-off garden in the centre of the square. Bodie tooled the Capri most neatly into a parking space, a rarity hereabouts like a whole ice-cream in Hell, and he and Doyle got out. They walked towards the little garden, along the path, and the man waiting for them looked at his wristwatch.

This man was chunky, strongly-built, square-shouldered. He wore a smart overcoat of an elegant blue-grey colour, with a velvet collar, and he carried a rolled umbrella. Both Doyle and Bodie knew that with that brolly George Cowley, the Chief of CI5, could have your guts out in a twinkling. Cowley's square, lined face betrayed no real annoyance and the curve of his lips indicated only impatience.

'You're late.'

Bodie and Doyle had the sense not to make a song and dance about excuses or apologies.

'For your information,' Cowley went on in his brisk way, his plummy voice with the faintest burr of a Northern accent enough to make anyone brace up. 'I have an appointment with the Minister in exactly ten minutes.'

He walked along the path and his two top agents fell in beside him. Under Cowley's arm was tucked a slim file in its manila cover.

'Your target is a man. I want him found as soon as possible.'

Cowley handed the file across to Bodie.

'Here are photographs and details.'

As he had not been handed the file, Ray Doyle said: 'What's the man's name?'

'Quinn.'

Bodie looked up from the file which he had flicked open and rapidly perused.

'Escaped from Repton at oh-eight-hundred hours today.'

Doyle half-turned. 'A mental patient, on the run for less than two hours?'

The implication in both Doyle's tone and words was obvious. Cowley ignored that. Had the job been one for the local police force the local police force would be dealing. Quod erat demonstrandum.

Bodie got that. He said: 'Er – what's the connection with CI5?'

They had reached the opposite railings, and Cowley stopped and turned to face his two agents. His face bore down on them, grim and hard, and his voice was uncompromising.

'The connection is very simple. I want him found.'

As he finished speaking Cowley lifted his hand in a signal.

His Rover 3.5, with Paula at the wheel, eased near-silently up from where it had been waiting. Cowley walked around the railings and across the strip of pavement. He opened the rear door and got in, slammed the door and the Rover pulled away. He did not look around or say another word.

Bodie and Doyle were left by the flowers of the little garden, by the railings.

Bodie sniffed. 'What's he been eating? Razor blades?'

'Yeah,' said Doyle. 'All the better to bite your head off.'

He jerked his thumb at the file in Bodie's hand.

'Anything in there?'

'Photos, personal description, bit about the break-out.'

Bodie's tones were flat. Doyle said: 'And?'

Bodie sniffed again and his famous lips wrinkled up into their famous grimace. 'And that's it. Nothing.'

Doyle did not look so much puzzled as resigned.

'So why is it so important to find this guy?'

Bodie moved his elegantly-clad shoulders. Doyle looked back to where the Capri was parked at the far end of the square. He took a florin from his pocket, spun it, clapped a hand over it as he caught it and transferred it to the back of his other hand.

'Call it.'

Bodie looked daggers; but said: 'Heads.'

Doyle lifted his hand and smiled.

'Tails. Go get the car.'

Out of the various houses available Quinn chose at random. Mock Tudor, the beams rather too ostentatious, the leaded windows rather too brittle, the roof just that much sharper than the genuine; all the same, this house smelt of money. There were extensive grounds. The surrounding walls were high; not that they stopped Quinn.

There was an Alsatian guard dog.

He stretched to the very extent of his chain, snarling, bristling, very ready to take a chunk out of anyone, including Quinn.

Quinn looked in a mess.

His sweat shirt was ripped, dried blood speckled him, his face looked like a map of the Amazon jungle. He crouched down before the dog, just out of range of those sharp savage teeth.

He made sucking clicking soothing noises.

The Alsatian barked, stopped, shook his head, barked again. He was not at all sure what was going on.

Slowly, Quinn extended his hand. Slowly, slowly . . .

The dog sniffed the hand, sniffed again, then whimpered. Quinn did not smile; but he reached forward with authority and stroked the dog's head.

'Good boy,' he said; now there was no need.

Quickly he undid the chain fastening the dog's collar. The Alsatian couldn't believe his luck, Delighted, he gave Quinn's hand a ferocious pleased lick and then lolloped away up the garden. Quinn watched him go and the creases between his eyes dented in for a moment.

Then he turned his full formidable attention on the house. A prowl around all four sides had given no indication of anyone being at home. He looked through a window into a perfectly ordinary room; moved along and checked the next. A typical well-off house, perhaps a little vulgar, no doubt crammed with goodies. He put an elbow through a window pane, unlocked it and shoved it open.

The lounge contained a built-in bar with a splendid array of bottles; easy chairs, an imitation-stone fireplace filled with an electric fire, standard lamps, were some of the furnishings. The place looked like a High Street furniture shop window. Above the bar a number of framed photographs showed boxers, usually with a glove well up to their chin and the other poking aggressively forward.

Quinn absorbed the information the room gave him, then moved easily into the hall. More furniture-shop products, and a deep carpet leading aloft. Thither, Quinn went.

The power with which he went up the stairs reflected his growing confidence. There was about this man something of the dangerous jungle animal, startled at the water hole, ready to tear and rend if provoked.

The master bedroom offered what he wanted.

He checked the en suite bathroom, searched the bedroom, working methodically. He was perfectly relaxed. It was clear he'd done this before. The wad of money, this time, turned up at the back of a drawer under a folded newspaper. Quinn tossed the wad into the air, caught it and then flipped it onto the bed. He took clothes from the wardrobe, examined them critically for size and fit; the style was not pleasing, and threw the selected garments onto the bed beside the notes.

Then he went into the bathroom to clean up.

The hot water was good, the scent of the soap and the feel of the suds soothing. He took his time cleaning up.

The sound of a car on the gravel did not bother him overmuch. He finished dressing in his own time.

Jack Canon was the kind of man who would own a house of this nature and run a big Mercedes. As he stopped the car and got out, his dog came lolloping up from the back, starting to slobber all over him.

Charley Harris, Canon's handyman cum companion, got out and walked around the car to grab the dog's collar.

'How'd the dog get loose?' demanded Canon. He looked suspiciously around, saw nothing amiss, and hurried to his house.

Canon had boxed professionally for ten years, and now, in his mid thirties, looked a hard, big man. Perhaps his colour was too high. Perhaps the veins at the sides of his nose were too blue-red and pronounced. Maybe he walked with too much of a swagger. All the same, a tough man, and a nasty fellow to cross. His companion, Harris, looked just as powerful in the physical sense.

They went in through the front door.

Canon stopped, staring up, and his mouth opened and his eyes half-closed. He didn't really believe what he was seeing, not in his own house.

Quinn was half way down the stairs. he looked clean and spruced up.

Canon shouted up: 'Who the hell are you?'

The sound of the shout, the authority in the words, the hint of punishment for misdeeds, abruptly cowed Quinn. Once more he was back in the institution, for treatment, watched, spied on, studied, kept sedated. He flinched back.

'He's only wearing one of my suits.' Canon sounded disgusted. He had this pretty little situation under control now. Some stupid light-fingered monkey – stupid enough to monkey with Jack Canon, who'd laid out Slugger Duvalier in two, and light-fingered and stupid enough to pinch one of Jack Canon's suits! 'Get down here! Come on down here, you.'

The words hammered at Quinn.

Slowly he descended the last few steps.

Canon reached out and grabbed him, pulled him down the last couple of steps.

'All right, sunshine. How'd you get in here?'

Harris called right away from the lounge.

'Jack –'

Canon gave Quinn a push on the shoulder to steer him along. Quinn moved like a robot. He moved obediently. The simple fact of unthinking authority imposed without question brought him back to the beginning. They went into the lounge.

'Oh,' said Canon in a disgusted voice. 'That's nice. That's charming, carpet full of broken glass.'

'I'll call the police,' said Harris.

'Hold on, hold on.' Canon's plug-ugly face broke into a smile. 'We can handle this. Get us a drink.'

He turned to Quinn. 'All right. What you got in those pockets?'

The feeling of suspense increased as Canon, the blood hot in him, could elicit no response from the intruder. He patted the pockets of the suit Quinn wore, Canon's own bloody suit! 'What d'you take? What you got?' He patted the other pockets now and, unconsciously, adopted the pose of a boxer. 'What's in there?' He sparred at the pockets of the suit, enjoying himself, taunting openly now, vicious. 'What's in that one?'

The barrage of little blows delivered with open fists drove Quinn back. He stumbled. One hand caught at the arm of a chair to steady himself. The other arm lifted in a quite automatic gesture to shield his face.

Canon's voice became hoarse.

'You thick or something, raising your fist to me?' Canon's

face flushed beetroot. His eyes glared. He felt the power in him. 'D'you know who I am?'

He grabbed Quinn's upraised arm, twisted, pushed the bent arm up Quinn's back. Subdued, Quinn was pushed headfirst towards the bar. Canon forced the big man's head up.

'See those, dummy. That's me.'

Quinn stared at the photographs. Canon was clearly recognisable as the flashy boxer with raised gloves.

But Quinn looked at the photograph, and saw, quite clearly. He saw the face of the doctor who had jabbed the hypo into him, the face of the Colonel in the K.G.B. wearing the high-collared uniform. Quinn saw that face and he reacted. He pulled free of the arm lock.

Canon allowed he felt a little surprise; but he was still angry.

'Get out of that suit,' he shouted. 'Come on, take it off.'

As the intruder glowered back in a very different way from the way he'd been behaving so far, more like a congenital idiot, Canon lost his temper. If this thief wouldn't take the suit off, then Jack Canon would take it off for him.

He leaped forward, grabbed the suit's lapels, and started to force the coat back off the big man's shoulders.

Quinn staggered, recovered, and then stiffened. His fist shot out, a short sudden jab to Canon's solar plexus. The ex-boxer doubled up and staggered back. But he was not hurt. He was angry now, coldly angry, determined to cut this monkey up.

He moved menacingly forward.

Harris called out. 'Leave it, Jack. I'll phone the police.'

'No.' Canon fairly snarled the words, cold and hard. 'We can take this monkey apart.'

With that Canon hurled himself forward, his fists doubled up, hard, knobby fists, that knew all the dirty punches in the book - and some that the book didn't know about.

Quinn avoided the rush and the flurry of blows, got in close, took Canon in a grip which upended him and with cunning expertise dumped him down on the coffee table.

The table collapsed into splinters. Harris let out a yell and rushed in bull-headed. He tore into Quinn from the side.

As Harris lunged forward, Quinn swayed, recovered, put a fist into his guts and as Harris doubled up chopped him down with a series of decisive palm-edgers that drove Harris nose-first into the carpet.

But Canon was up on his feet, free of the coffee table wreckage. He circled this big man, suddenly wondering if he'd had such a good idea. He glanced at the fireplace. The electric fire was out, and the fancy fake heavy brass companion set glittered. Canon reached. He picked up the brass poker. The head was well-polished. Canon weighed it up and down, letting it drop with a splat into his open palm. He stalked towards Quinn, once more confident.

Abruptly, using all the explosive skill conferred from his ring experience allied to boxer's legs still in trim, Canon charged. He swung the heavy brass poker with murderous power. The brass caught the light from the windows and glittered as it lashed down – just as an axe head had caught the sunlight and splintered a star . . .

Quinn avoided the blow with a smooth action, let the man's own momentum carry him on, long experience with sadistic guards and their bludgeons telling him how long he had to take this one. The blow whistled past harmlessly. Quinn chopped the man across the bridge of the nose and with his power and control surged the blow on to impact behind the left ear.

On the carpet Harris lay groaning.

Jack Canon fell to lie unconscious.

Quinn stared down on them both for a moment. Then he shrugged his new suit straight and went out.

The white Capri whistled down the street as Doyle, having secured the file from Bodie, flipped it open on his knee and read what meagre information there was.

Driving with his relaxed skill, Bodie said from the corner of his mouth: 'What was he wearing?'

'Sweat shirt, slacks, old pair of trainers.'

'Did he have any money?'

'No.'

Bodie grimaced, indicating both pity and satisfaction in equal proportions.

'Well, he can't get far like that.'

Doyle rapped the file. 'So, where does he go to? What does he do?'

'What would you do?' Bodie nodded to the R/T. 'Gee 'em up again.'

Doyle picked up the handset and called out.

'4.5 to base. Anything shown yet on the police reports? We're still interested in any break-in around the Repton area . . .'

The operator – it sounded like that curly-haired kid with the snaky chassis they called Tina – replied.

'Nothing shown up. You'll be informed.'

'We'll be informed,' Doyle said to Bodie as he replaced the set. 'When, I'd like to know.'

'Like always,' said Bodie, smoothly turning the wheel, his face smooth with aftershave, his eyelids half-lowered as he drove, his chin up, a smooth operative all around, Bodie. 'Like always, old son. When it's almost too late.'

'One of these days it's going to be too late –'

The R/T cheeped and Doyle rather more vigorously than he intended, yanked the set and said: '4.5'

'4.5. Break-in reported in area of interest. Description of the intruder fits, and the location is near the clinic. Address: Jackie Canon's place, Oaklands, Norris Way, South West, a big make-believe Tudor place.'

'Right,' said Doyle. 'On our way. 4.5. out.'

Bodie checked the rear view mirror and hauled out of the line of traffic to speed up and overtake on the outside lane. There was no need for a dramatic U-turn, all skidding and screeching tyres, for, quite obviously, they were on their way to Repton and therefore pointing in the right direction. Mind you, Bodie quite missed the flair of those exciting U-turns . . .

Not so George Cowley, chief of CI5. He bent to his own R/T in the back of his Rover, and his voice for all its plummy richness carried acid overtones.

'Anything on 3.7 or 4.5.?'

The R/T operative's voice spoke up in reply at once. Tina knew she was dealing with the big man himself.

'Yes, sir. On their way to a break-in two miles from Repton.'

'What was taken?'

'Clothing and money, sir. Two hundred pounds.'

Cowley did not reply for a moment, sitting in the back of his Rover, thinking. He passed a hand across his chin. He had to run a department - bureau, organisation, call it what you will - set up by governmental authority, to fight crime by all the means at modern forensic science's disposal, plus methods used by the criminals themselves, and still it all boiled down to men and decisions.

'Right,' he said, at last, back to form, crisp and no-nonsense George Cowley. 'Tell 3.7 and 4.5 to contact me at the clinic.'

The R/T operative's voice sounded oddly meek.

'Yes, sir.'

Maybe Tina was just relieved to be let off the hook. You had to try to keep level with Cowley by running as fast as you could, and even then he was usually one jump ahead of you. All, for an R/T operator, all metaphorically speaking, of course.

As Cowley headed for the clinic, Bodie tooled the white Capri along Norris Way. They spotted Oaklands, and Bodie said: 'Now that's a house -'

And Doyle said: 'Little plastic gnome-men, maybe.'

They rolled up the drive and got out and looked at the police car already standing to one side. The locals were on the job. Their CI5 credentials got them past the bobby on the door and into the lounge. A forensic team was dusting, looking for prints. The officer in charge nodded to his sergeant as the two CI5 men ambled in. Let the flash boys get finished, he seemed to be saying, and then we can get on with the real work.

Bodie vaguely remembered Canon.

Jackie Canon sat on the sofa holding an ice bag to his face and looking sizzlingly angry and profoundly miserable at the same time, which is quite a trick. Bodie was in no mood to play games.

'Don't tell me he put you down, Champ.'

Canon didn't reply; but the ice-bag twitched.

Doyle shoved a photo of Quinn under Canon's nose.

'Was this the man?'

Canon looked. The ice bag twitched again.

'Yeah. That's him.'

Doyle nodded to Harris who sat in the armchair nursing his arm, which was smothered in a large bandage. 'And,' said Doyle, in a voice he tried to keep neutral and which still could not conceal the lilt of laughter underlying just about all the words Ray Doyle spoke: 'And he did you both up?'

The ice bag shook.

Canon looked up, his face ugly from bruising and anger.

'Man was a nutter. Lunatic. Four of us would have had a job to hold him.'

'You'd better get back in training.'

Canon flared up.

'Training! He'd been trained all right. Commando or something. Trained to kill - with his bare hands.'

The look Bodie and Doyle exchanged meant more than one thing; but one thing it meant was that they had learned something about this mysterious Quinn for whom they were searching. He was a man trained to kill.

The street was not so much seedy as merely run down. Stucco peeling from brickwork on some fronts, freshly white-washed on others; some doors looking like leprous fungi, others painted up in bright colours; some windows clean, others dirty. The house with the 'Bedsit Vacant' accommodation Quinn chose seemed to lie between the two extremes. The steps were dirty at street level; but the door-sill was freshly done over. The landlady appeared a string-bundle of sticks, hard, ascetic, used to awkward customers, and anxious only to have the rent in her hand week by week.

She showed him up the linoleum covered stairs and pushed the door open. The smells in the house were not too intrusive; dust, cabbage, furniture polish, and, incongruously, a strong smell of marmalade.

As Quinn looked around the small room, the landlady folded her arms over the bundle of sticks she called a bosom under the black dress.

'Here we are. It's the only one empty at the moment.'

Quinn saw the bed, of pale oak - or orange-crate stained - the heavy old-fashioned wardrobe which was probably really old and heavy and big and therefore wanted by no one, a tiny stove by the sink in the corner, the hang of the curtains, chintzy material long past its prime.

'It's thirty pounds a week. Payable in advance. The gas meter's under the sink.'

Quinn just didn't react to the sales talk.

The landlady gave a hitch to herself, licked her lips and went on: 'The facilities are down the passage on the right.'

Still Quin looked about. What the woman was saying did not appear to register. She spoke more sharply.

'You are English?'

This brought Quinn's attention to life.

'Huh - yes.'

'Well, as I said. It's thirty a week. Payable in advance.'

Quinn brought out some money, for he had broken the wad up as a mere precaution, and paid off six fivers. The landlady took the money with the ease of long practice. She gave Quinn a look of that nose-lifted, disdainful kind that suggested she deserved a medal for suffering such a cretin of a lodger.

When the door closed Quinn shook his shoulders. He shut his eyes and then opened them, quickly. He crossed to the door and locked it. He checked it was locked, testing the handle, and then removed the key. Crossing to the sink he ran the water, turned the tap off, turned it on again, turned it off. He caught sight of the items on the scrap of draining board.

One was an empty plastic container of washing-up liquid. The other item was a tin of boot polish. Quinn turned the key and opened it. Blacking. He threw the tin down and went over to the window.

This was of the sash variety. The sash cords were probably as old as Queen Victoria, fragile and rotten with age, the weights hanging by a thread. The wood had swollen. Quinn got his fingers under the grips and heaved. After a bit of silent struggle, his strength overcame the stiffness of the window frame. It lifted with a squeal. He forced it up, then pulled it down. After a couple of movements up and down the window ran more freely. Quinn closed it down.

The big heavy ornamental wardrobe was empty. As he gripped it, one hand up to the corner angle, the other down to the opposite angle, and heaved, Quinn recognised the thing *was* heavy. He managed to heave it along from corner to corner, rocking it, turning it so that it ended up canted across the corner of the room. It blocked off a triangle of floor into the angle. He pushed the door shut.

He looked around. He appeared to be satisfied with his work.

The covers on the bed were drawn up. They looked like enormous violet roses, garishly entwined. Quinn lay on the bed and stretched out on the bed of violet roses. He stared up at the ceiling with unseeing eyes.

How long elapsed after that between the time Quinn closed his eyes and the time he opened them in overwhelming panic he could not say. The room lay in semi-darkness from the drawn curtains. Quinn lay, sweating, glaring up helplessly.

Suddenly, he reached up and pulled the knob dangling at the end of its string and the bare bulb dangling at the end of its wire burst into yellow light.

At once Quinn flinched back.

The light drove daggers into his eyes. His face screwed up. An inner conflict of enormous proportions began, reflected in his face, in the sweat, in the way his mouth twisted and spittle ran down the creases in his chin.

He mewed in terror.

The voice of the First Interrogator, hollow, echoing, drummed in Quinn's tortured mind.

'Why do you resist? Why do you fight it? You know we will break you sooner or later.'

Now Quinn knew he was strapped in the interrogation room. The searing blaze of light beat relentlessly into his face, his eyes. There was no escape. Voices spilled from the darkness beyond the lights.

The Second Interrogator spoke, his voice higher, colder, than the First Interrogator's, like a snake's hiss.

'You may hold out for another day, another week. But do you think anyone cares? Do you imagine your people in London are at all concerned about you now?'

The mental agony of the ordeal tortured Quinn. He lay, feeling the straps encircling his wrists and ankles, feeling the heat of the arc lights blazing into his face, unable to escape from the nightmare.

'Be sensible, Quinn.' The voice of the First Interrogator from beyond the wall of light appeared to soothe, to appeal to reason. The hollow words bounced around inside Quinn's skull. 'They sent you knowing the risk. They sent you because to them, you are ... *expendable.*'

As the First Interrogator's words echoed to silence, the Second Interrogator leaned into the spill of light. He leered down on Quinn. His face was the face of the guard who had grabbed for his leg as Quinn went over the wall. The viciousness of the face leered on Quinn, sweating on his bed of pain.

The first face was joined by a second, seeming to hang suspended and disembodied in the reflected light.

This was the face of Doctor Krasnov, who had injected Quinn, who spoke so soothingly of betrayal and death and expendability ...

Quinn sucked in a huge draught of air.

He whooped with effort. He struggled to rise.

With a supreme effort he dragged himself off the bed and lurched towards the window. He reached up half-blind and wrenched the curtains open. Daylight flooded in.

For a long time he stood there, hands on the curtains, head hanging, sucking draughts of air. It took him a long time to return to a semblance of normality, to the real world of the bedsitting room.

Presently he stumbled back to the bed and pulled the knob on its string and extinguished the light.

He noticed his hand was smeared with something black.

He looked puzzled.

Then, on the wall, he saw more black smears.

He looked more closely. On the wall in large shaky capital letters four names were scrawled.

GRANGER. HOWARD. LENISTON. MORRIS.

He walked across to the wall. On the floor by the paint-flaking wainscotting lay the tin of black boot polish. Quinn picked it up. He looked at the black stuff on his hand, at the tin of polish, at the names on the wall.

He shook his head. He had no memory - no memory of writing the names on the wall. But the blacking from the tin was on his hand, the names scrawled across the wall.

Quinn did not know how he felt. His thoughts were confused. There were imperatives, all pushing him. There were things he had to do, things he *must* do. His brains were in turmoil.

He threw the tin down, plodded for the door, unlocked it and went out.

A man named Quinn was on the loose.

At the Repton Clinic young Doctor Armstrong wore a worried frown under his mop of fair hair. He fiddled with the stethoscope slung around his neck. He and George Cowley walked down the corridor and turned right-handed into the waiting room. They went through into Doctor Howard's surgery.

Cowley looked around and then crossed to the ruins of the window through which Quinn had hurled himself in a frenzy of - a frenzy of what?

Doctor Armstrong shook his head at Cowley's obvious query.

'Sad to think a man like Quinn should be so reduced. Just a muscle beach-hulk. That's what he was. Physically in perfect trim.' Armstrong fingered his stethoscope. 'Mentally . . .'

Cowley nodded. 'Tuned out.'

'Think of the mind as a computer. Then, somehow, the power is disconnected, switched off. In layman's terms the patient becomes isolated from reality, suspended in a kind of limbo.' Doctor Armstrong resented the futility of much of his work; but he kept on trying. 'We were trying to reverse the process.'

'Reconnecting the computer?' said Cowley. 'Switching on again?'

'Yes. But there was little progress.'

Cowley walked across to the window and swung around to face Armstrong.

'Doctor. Have you any idea what would make Quinn dive out of this window?'

'I would be guessing . . . But if he received some mental

stimulant, some shock strong enough to bring him back to reality – '

'Reality?' Cowley's interruption came sharply.

Armstrong lifted a hand. 'Perhaps – perhaps only partial. Perhaps only real for Quinn – '

Even as he tried to indicate the kind of half-life he anticipated lay ahead of Quinn no matter what had happened to him, a male nurse ran in through the opened doorway. He was out of breath, running, his boots loud. He did not wait before speaking.

'Doctor . . . A body . . . We've found a body . . . '

Armstrong looked shocked and Cowley, professionally, took over. Under his calm promptings the orderly quietened down and led them outside and around to the rear quarters and towards the detached boiler house. At one side, tall galvanised refuse containers stood beyond the pile of coke. Some of the coke was scattered about as though a demented truck driver had tipped his load on a drunken spree. Cowley, Doctor Armstrong and the male nurse hurried towards the door of the boiler house. Coke crunched underfoot.

The male nurse hung back, pointing.

Cowley peered down to where some of the coke had been shovelled aside. The big coke shovel lay there, black and silver, abandoned. Cowley, still bent over, said: 'Who is it?'

The doctor bent beside Cowley, staring. His face looked abruptly horrified.

'My God! It's Grey – Doctor Grey.'

Doctor Grey had a dark moustache, plastered across his swarthy face, and sleek black hair. His face was entirely different from the face of the Doctor Grey who had given Quinn the injection.

The corpse's face looked bloated, and Cowley suspected forensic would merely confirm what he had already seen.

The white Capri tooled up along the road and by the time Bodie and Doyle, reporting in, as instructed, reached their chief, there was little to do but call the ambulance and order the flowers.

Cowley regarded them bleakly.

'Now it's not just a break-out,' said Cowley. 'Now it's a killing.'

Doyle with his ex-policeman's instincts running, bent over to look at the dead man.

'Strangled with a cheese-wire.'

Bodie sniffed.

'Quick - not entirely painless.'

The three men from CI5 looked at one another.

Just what it was all about, so far, Bodie and Doyle had no idea. But, now, they had been told, Quinn, the man they had to find, was a killer trained to kill. And now - cheesewire? Had they found an example of his handiwork?

From the bedsit Quinn found his way out of town and into the woods with an ease and familiarity that did not puzzle him. He knew where to go and what to do and there was no mystery about it to him.

The woods lay under the sun, quiet and deserted of human life before Quinn stepped between the trees. Now his resemblance to a sleek, ferocious, hunting animal became even more pronounced. He looked the trained killer he was.

The sunshine cast little patternings of light between and through the leaves, gold and green. Quinn looked at the trees, moving quietly, until he came to a large and distinctively shaped tree which, by virtue of its age and size, had created for itself a little extra space among the crowding young stems. Here Quinn stopped. He moved with purpose when at last he walked to the tree, turned, placed his back squarely against it and paced off four even strides. He dug his heel into the soft, mossy ground beside a partially-exposed root.

He started with his hands, then found a stick, and very quickly he had excavated deeply enough to reveal the handles of the holdall. He scraped loose earth away, took the handles, heaved, and like a championship fish coming clear of the water, the holdall flew up out of the hole.

Quinn unbuckled the holdall. His hands were perfectly steady. He acted as though he was a programmed robot without a thought for anything, apart from what it was doing.

Thick plastic wrapped an object. Quinn dragged the plastic off, to reveal a light assault rifle. The metal of the gun gleamed blue.

He clicked out the folding butt. The front section of the barrel was detachable. The holdall contained magazines in plastic pouches. Quinn took one out. He clipped it into the underside of the assault rifle. He stood up. He gripped the rifle with the precise hold of a man who knew what he was doing.

Then, with a yell, he pressed the trigger and cut a fusillade of high-velocity bullets through the surrounding trees. Like a maniac, he whirled around, firing, firing, firing . . .

The magazine spat the last round, the rifle was empty.

But the killing machine they called Quinn was ready . . .

Chapter Two

CI5, the Squad, the Big A, maintained a few discreetly hidden cars under dustsheets in lock-ups or mouldy old warehouses. Also, Bill Johnson, a big fellow with a quiff of fair hair and grease smudged all over him, ran a quick-service repair shop in a side street that was so quiet you could hear the grass growing in the cracks of the paving flags. Where the oil from damaged sumps hadn't run, that was.

From outside, the yard looked a mess, with oil barrels stacked alongside old tyres. If the barrels hadn't fallen to pieces through rust it was only because they had once carried oil. If the tyres had been any balder they'd have ceased to exist, treadwise, as some might say.

Once Quinn walked smoothly past the entrance, though, the situation changed. A great deal of modern equipment in perfect working condition stood against the far wall. There was a hum of power, and the feeling of efficiency. Bill Johnson liked to put on a good sloppy cover, and he more than liked to run a tight shop. He demanded it.

This place existed for CI5 men to come to in emergency and they always knew that a set of wheels would be ready on the line.

Quinn had tried two of the lock-ups he'd known in the old days. One was now a launderette. The other had been the scene of a little high-rolling and pot-smoking, and the young gentry involved had incontinently fled when Quinn stuck his powerful frame around the door.

Now he eased up to Johnson.

Bill squinted up against the light through the open doorway, seeing the man as a silhouette.

'Can I help you?'

'I need a car.'

'Sorry,' said Johnson, not quickly, just the right amount

of casual speed. 'We just do repair work – ' He looked more closely at the man, turning his head to get a better view. The truth dawned. 'Quinn!'

Johnson moved forward and sideways. No doubt, now.

'My God, it is. Quinn. I thought you were – I mean, the last I heard – '

Quinn shook his head.

'Well I'm back.'

'Right.' Johnson took a swab out of his dungaree pockets. 'It's great to see you again.'

'What,' said Quinn, now the politenesses were out of the way, 'about the car?'

'Sure.' Johnson didn't like the look of Quinn now he could see him more clearly. And it had been a damned long time ago. And if it wasn't dead, Quinn had been reported, then – in his line of work – it had been worse.

'Sure,' he said again, making it hearty. 'We can fix you up.'

Quinn nodded and looked around, finally pointed at one of the cars. 'That'll do.'

'Yeah, fine.' Johnson wasn't nervous – why should he be? – but his voice sounded a bit off. 'It's got a good engine. I'll check it right through, you can pick it up in a couple of days.'

Quinn began to move towards the car.

'I'll take it now.'

'Hold it a minute.' Johnson ran around the job he'd been working on to get between Quinn and the car he'd chosen. 'Look – you can't just walk in here after all this time . . . ' The look in Quinn's face was now clearly menacing. Most clearly. 'I need authorisation. I need to check, you know that.'

Quinn nodded and some of the grimness left him.

'You check it, Johnson.'

Johnson gave the big man a smile. Something very close and potentially hairy had been going down there for a minute or two. He walked over to the phone. He dialled out, his back to Quinn.

When the car's engine started up, Johnson whirled and began to run for it, waving his arms and shouting.

But, somehow, he wasn't really surprised.

Quinn hit the accelerator and gunned the car straight for the open doorway. Trouble, although no trouble for Quinn, was that only one door was open.

Quinn just drove the car slap bang through the door and took away a sizeable section of wood with him. The car rocked on its springs, splinters and chips flew. From the window at Repton Clinic, Quinn had now moved up to garage doors. He was growing more spectacular.

A car trundling along this quiet street was forced to swerve and brake violently. The man inside, shaking and with a white face, stared sickly after the maniac's car as it howled away up the road.

Now a man called Quinn had wheels.

George Cowley felt he would never properly develop a system by which he could conduct interviews of the type which now confronted him. Quinn's wife - ex-wife - Teresa, ran a small bookshop and was making a new life.

In her early forties, Teresa Quinn looked older. She barely looked up as Cowley entered the shop.

'Can I help you?'

'Do you have a copy of "My University" by Kim Philby?'

'I don't think we - ' She looked up and saw Cowley and - it was quick, really - recognised him. 'George Cowley.'

'Have I changed that much?'

'No.' Teresa Quinn remembered the laconic wit of the old Cowley. 'No, you haven't. If anything, you look trimmer.'

'Two piece suits and obligatory calisthenics. You look well, - Teresa -'

'I look the way I deserve; black coffee, white wine and an addiction to milk chocolate to get me through the long afternoons. The book trade isn't exactly booming.'

'So I'm told.'

'If there's one product a country can't afford to let go down the drain, that product is the book; all right!' She spoke defiantly. 'With a capital bloody B! Book!' Cowley wasn't listening; but she finished. 'No price is too expensive to pay for a book. Because the alternative means prices don't mean anything any more.'

After a moment, Cowley said: 'Quinn's on the loose.'

Teresa put a hand to her throat.

'From Repton? How could he get *out* of there?'

Cowley was not prepared to answer that directly. 'I think we all thought he was finished - broken - he'd become a fixture. Quiet, docile, harmless . . . Do you still go to see him?'

Teresa lowered her eyes. 'George, I - look, I know it's a platitude; but life goes on. It became pointless. Heart-breaking. He won't last five minutes.'

'The sooner he's back, the better for him - '

'The better for you, you mean!' Anger broke from Teresa Quinn. 'He'd be impressed - if he had a mind, that is - to know that you, George, Alpha himself, had stirred himself to come looking. I didn't know you were visible any more! I didn't know you came out from behind your computers, your memory banks, your technology, to show a human face. It must be important!'

Cowley said: 'They broke him. Not us.' He spoke heavily, dully. 'We want him back.'

'Yes, yes. You'll have him back if he comes to me - '

She was approaching the breaking point in this conversation. Cowley saw it all - he'd seen it before, and knew he'd see it again, and so, to finish he said: 'The doctor who looked after him was strangled . . . '

Teresa turned her head away, as though slapped around the cheek. 'Oh, God. Get out, George. I know how to dial nine nine nine . . . '

Cowley turned and went out.

The bookshop bell tinkled away to silence.

Back in his Rover, Cowley refused to contemplate his share of the crimes attributable to heads of departments. Of whatever nations and in whatever times. Pontius Pilate must have been a departmental head. He reached for the radio.

'Alpha.'

The operative told him what had happened at the garage, of Bill Johnson's report of the misapprehended car.

'Right. Circulate the registration number. I want that car found.'

He replaced the handset and sat back on the seat.

To himself, echoing what he had just said on the R/T, he said: 'I want Quinn found.'

After that there was the next obvious port of call.

'Colonel Granger's house.' He spoke to his driver and Paula braced up. 'As fast as you like.'

During the drive to Granger's house, which was set by the river with well-kept gardens sweeping down to the Thames, Cowley fretted over how little he knew. He had those two, Bodie and Doyle, out sniffing around. But he wanted to know what had triggered Quinn . . .

Colonel Granger was taking a stroll in his gardens when Cowley stepped out of the Rover and walked across to join him. Granger had the face of a bull-pup, with a brushed moustache and bloodshot eyes. He was wise enough to try to stop himself from saying: 'What? What?' at the end of every other sentence. He wore a pepper and salt and carried a shooting stick, and he was most interested in his flower beds. The damned gardener seemed to think he owned the roses instead of Granger.

He said to Cowley after the amenities: 'Nice of you to come by, George; but it wasn't to see the roses.'

'No, it wasn't. I assume you've heard about Quinn?'

'Yes. Had a call. Try to keep an ear to the ground, especially if it concerns any of the old boys.'

'To be frank, I'm worried.'

Granger brushed his moustache. 'Then so am I, George.'

Cowley paced at the side of the colonel, who half bent his head attentively. 'I have a theory,' said Cowley, 'or at least the beginnings of a theory.'

'Dangerous things, theories, like gut reactions and intuitions.'

Cowley knew Granger meant well, that this was just his manner. 'Perhaps I'm too close, too involved.'

Granger nodded wisely. 'It's been a bad year, too much rain.' He saw that young Cowley wasn't really listening. 'Why don't you,' said Colonel Granger with great magnanimity, 'expound your theory?'

And, as the two men walked in the sunshine across the lawns sweeping down to the Thames, Quinn's head and shoulders rose stealthily into view among the shrubbery.

He saw the two men, the set up, the way the sun threw shadows, the lie of the land. Then he rapidly screwed the assault rifle together, clipped out the folding butt. He checked the scope mounting. He worked with his hands on jobs like this in the way of a man who knew exactly what he was doing. No matter what nationality the equipment.

He snugged the rifle and peered through the scope.

Cowley came into focus, and then Granger, walking along together. The cross wires centred on Granger. Quinn's forefinger began to tighten – and Granger walked past beyond a bush. All Quinn could see to shoot at were shiny green leaves.

The look on Quinn's face reflected relief . . .

Then Cowley and Granger walked past the bush. Once more they were targets. Quinn centred the cross hairs on Granger.

He fought a tangle of thoughts all colliding and jumping in his head. The indecision reached him like a carillon of bells falling from a church steeple razed by high-explosive. He had a job to do, and there were these men, and the clouds boiled up to obscure what he would or could think of . . . He took careful aim at Granger. Granger was one of the names . . .

Quinn's indecision ended. He pressed the trigger.

The bullet hit Colonel Granger in his left side, penetrated his heart and smashed to damnation on a rib on his right side. The colonel fell. Cowley hit the grass in the split second another shot cracked out. The bullet sizzled through air where a second before Cowley had been standing.

Quinn simply blundered backwards, turning, haring for the river and the riverbank path.

Cowley took a breath, leaped up. He looked down on Granger. The man lay with his face sideways on to the turf; the fierce upthrust moustache still jutted arrogantly; the jaw still thrust foward as defiantly; but he was dead.

Cowley looked towards the shrubbery just in time to catch a fleeting glimpse of a man running. Instantly, Cowley started off. The bullet in his leg pained him; he limped; but despite that he covered the ground. That bullet had been put there by a gunner of the Condor Legion and no surgeon would risk Cowley's leg to take it out; so Cowley put up with the pain, and limped, but kept his leg.

By the time he reached the river, bursting out onto the path, there was no sight of Quinn to be seen.

Quinn had simply belted, head down, the rifle swinging, hurtled along the path and back again through the side of the shrubbery and so back to the road. He could have gone either way on the riverbank path, and either way again from the shrubbery. All pursuit thrown off, Quinn slowed down. He took the rifle to pieces and stowed it in the bag. Then he walked to where he'd stashed the car under the trees. The birds were singing. Nothing else made any noise, until Quinn started the car. Before that he held his hands to his head, hunched over the steering wheel, getting his breath back. But he was getting over more than a quick run along a riverbank path.

Finally he sat up, started the car, and drove away.

When he let himself back into his bedsit he looked around the room carefully. Nothing had changed. He closed and locked the door and, for an instant, leaned back against it as though for support. He put the bag with the broken-down assault rifle under the bed. Then he crossed to the sink and ran the cold water tap.

He splashed water into his face.

His own fatigue, the single light, the water hitting his face with cutting shock ...

The hollow echoing voice of the First Interrogator blasted about him.

'The names, Quinn.'

Quinn was there, swaying on his feet, almost out and the thrown water from the jug snapping him awake, awake to the lights and the uniforms and the harsh words.

'The names, Quinn. What are the names?'

'I've told you a thousand times ... '

'We want to make sure you remember. *The names!*'

Mumbling, Quinn recited the litany.

'Granger ... Howard ... Leniston ... '

Quinn's voice tailed away.

'One more.' The Interrogator made it harsh, authoritative, unyielding. 'One more. What is the last name?'

'Morris.'

'And what do you do to the names?'

Quinn was shaking his head. He tried to think and could not, trying to reject the names, the lights, the uniforms. 'I need to sleep. I must ... sleep ... '

'Tell me. Then you can sleep.'

The hollow voice circled in Quinn's head. He had to, had to ...

'I – I – ' mumbled Quinn. Then, with a spurt like the sputtering of a machine gun, he rattled out: 'I get the gun ... and the ammo ... and I kill them ... one by one ... '

He shuddered, standing there with the water drops on his face, reliving the nightmare. Then he rushed to the window and hauled the curtains across. He was still shaking.

He crossed to the wall where the names were scrawled.

He found the tin of blacking.

He stuck his forefinger in the tin of black boot polish. He drew the tip of that forefinger down through the first name. GRANGER. He used the same forefinger that had squeezed the trigger that had removed the real Granger, not just his name. That fitted.

Sitting astride his bike just at the corner of Angel Street and Gainsforth Road, Bill Eversely saw the Cortina go whisking past.

Nothing special about that car, but the number confirmed that this was the Cortina a routine obbo and report notice called for instant action. He started up and reported in, then took off. He followed the car to a quiet side road full of run-down boarding houses, noted the right one, and reported in again.

All in a day's work, reflected Bill Eversely.

He thought of his run-in with those two CI5 whizz-kids. Highly unlikely they'd stoop so low as to doing a bit of the old pinched-car reporting. That would be far too demeaning for them, if he wasn't doing them an injustice. Bill Eversely, thinking once more of Gloria, kicked his bike into life and went back to resume his station.

George Cowley did not move a muscle of his face as he

watched Granger's body, covered with a red blanket, carried away on the stretcher. The sun shone, the birds sang, and the world was short of a fierce brushed moustache and bloodshot eyes and the occasional: 'What? What?'

Bodie joined his chief.

He held out a bullet which he had retrieved from the sloping bank in line with the shrubbery and the spot Cowley had occupied. Bodie shook his head, sucking in his cheeks, looking dyspeptic.

'That one almost had your name on it, sir.'

Cowley did not reply but took the round. He was as well aware as anyone that Bodie was trying to be tactful and show his concern. Bodie ploughed on in the best Bodie head-up bash-on-regardless doomed way: 'It might help if you told us a little more about the man who fired it.'

Cowley looked at Bodie with his own Cowley look that could break armour plate at a thousand yards. Bodie understood quite well what the chief was saying. What Cowley did say, handing the bullet back to Bodie, was: 'Get it over to forensic.'

Doyle walked up the sloping lawns from the river.

'Nothing.' He shook his head. 'He's good.'

Thoughtfully, Cowley said: 'The best.'

He started to walk away, as though that was the most natural thing to do. Bodie looked most upset. He called after the chief of CI5.

'Sir! About Quinn ... '

Cowley stopped walking. He looked back, half-turning, then making up his mind.

'All right. Quinn was ... is ex-Special Forces. As a matter of fact we were operational together ... Field agents, before your time.'

It was not difficult for Cowley to remember. There were many men, there had been many men, with whom he had trained and laughed and kidded, and then served operationally in the field. Some of them remained good friends. A lot, a sickeningly horrific lot, were dead. And Quinn was – well, big Quinn was a man with whom Cowley had shared a few hairy moments. And the last one had been different again ...

'There was a defector, a big fish with important information. Quinn was assigned to get him out. It was a high rank mission. The defector was brought out, but – '

Cowley looked away from Bodie and Doyle. He went on his plummy voice hard now with remembered pain.

'But Quinn was taken, captured. The KGB had him for three years. Then he was exchanged. But he'd been broken mentally. He came back a shell.'

No one spoke for a pause long enough to make it represent something, a gesture, perhaps, to Quinn? A gesture, if that was the case, certainly futile. Then Doyle spoke.

'When was that?'

'Five years ago.'

They turned and began to walk back towards the house. The roses really were splendid.

'Since then he's been held in various clinics. Physically he's in perfect health. Mentally, he's a vegetable. There, but for the grace of God – go any one of us.'

The thought sobered Bodie and Doyle.

Not only that – Cowley's sombre words made them see the depth of Cowley's feelings for Quinn.

Doyle's bleeper bleeped.

'4.5.'

The operative's voice from the little R/T handset reached Doyle; and he nodded. 'The Cortina has been sighted. Parked Manston Street – '

Cowley regarded Doyle with a baleful eye.

'Well?' said the Chief of CI5. 'What are you waiting for?'

Bodie and Doyle stepped off the distance to their car very smartly. Very. When the old man made that kind enquiry, you responded smartly. Very.

Into his R/T Doyle said: 'Tell the locals to give it a wide berth now they've located it. Good work. We're on our way.'

The Capri tooled them there in short order and Bodie drove gently around the corner. They spotted the Cortina parked up an alley. Doyle nodded at the house.

'There it is. Place is a roomer – not altogether salubrious.'

'Better than some.'

Bodie drove past the house and found a place to pull in.

He admitted his luck. Finding holes in which to park these days was getting harder than finding unmelted ice creams in Hell. They alighted and walked back, Doyle making for the front door as Bodie headed for the back.

Up the steps Doyle reached for the bell at the same instant as the landlady opened the door. She was dressed, to go out, a decent coat over the bundle of sticks despite the sun. She carried a basket and was quite clearly going shopping.

With an echo of his old politeness as a police officer, Doyle said: 'Good afternoon.'

'If it's the ad you've come about,' said the landlady, drawing up her basket defensively. 'I'm afraid you've had a wasted journey. Full up. Could have taken you but I'm full up.'

Doyle took out his I.D.

'No. It's not about the room.'

The landlady saw the card. Her reaction was one of fascinated horror combined with incredulous disbelief that this was happening to her. She had always kept one of the most respectable houses in the street, always had, for years . . .

'Let's move inside, shall we?' suggested Doyle.

Inside the hall he closed the door quietly and then produced a photograph of Quinn.

'This one of your guests?'

The landlady put her hand to her mouth, and spoke as it were through the protection of splayed fingers.

'Top of the stairs. Room facing you – '

A sound at her back made her spin about as though about to be leapt on. Bodie walked into the hall from the back areas of the house.

The landlady let out a squeak.

'Take it easy,' said Doyle. 'Just stay down here. All right?' He spoke soothingly; but he put a little of the old snap into his voice, all the same. The landlady stared at them wide-eyed. Bodie gave her one of his smiles.

'And put the kettle on . . .'

They padded silently up the linoleum-covered stairs.

Bodie put his ear to the door of the room the landlady had indicated. Doyle went silently along the short passageway, found nothing, came back. He looked at Bodie. Bodie's smooth-featured face grew tense, a grimness flared his nostrils; they weren't play-acting now.

Inside the room Quinn lay on the bed staring sightlessly at the ceiling. He was a trained operative, one of the best, a man George Cowley had been pleased to go into the field with. Yes, his brains had been addled, he was a mental mess; but much of his training stuck. Much of his survival instinct operated on the levels below cerebral thought processes; the primitive aptitudes of the thalamus played a part. Quinn sat up. He looked towards the door.

Outside that door the two CI5 men slowly drew their guns.

They'd given up the Browning Hi-Powers of late, going into revolvers, and now they were carrying Smith and Wesson .41 magnums, packing a more powerful punch than the .357 and more handy than the .44. It was an experiment. Bodie, in particular, being the rifleman of the team, hankered after more than a measly six shots per load. Although Doyle, the handgun expert, always twitted him about one being enough - if you aimed it straight.

Once more they exchanged a look, shiny from Bodie, rough from Doyle. Together, they hit the door, smashed it off its hinges and sprang through.

In the same instant, it seemed, they were crouched on the floor, handguns aimed in the grip, covering every part of the bedsitting room.

There was no sign of Quinn.

The partners began fast, concentrated movements.

Bodie checked the window, drew the curtains, saw the window was still closed.

Doyle cased under the bed and around the sink - nothing.

They moved with controlled, precise movements, knowing what they were doing. The room was clean, except for the wardrobe.

The door was slightly ajar.

Bodie nodded to Doyle, face concentrated, and aimed his weapon. Doyle reached out, with a swift, sudden movement tugged the door open.

A single look convinced each man the wardrobe was empty.

No Quinn, no rifle - nothing . . .

They slumped back their handguns drooping, and with an almighty roar the wardrobe hurtled over and smashed down on top of them.

In a smother of action the two CI5 men went crumbling down under the weight of the massive wardrobe. Quinn surged up from the corner where he'd concealed himself in the triangular space, surged up and over the wardrobe. He carried his assault rifle as though going into Stalingrad. He hurdled the flattened door and vanished down the stairs.

Muffled, incoherent, but hot, very hot language announced the dishevelled disentanglement of two top CI5 agents from the wreck of the wardrobe.

They crawled to their feet.

Doyle's mop of curly hair looked dusted with flour, Bodie's tie was up under an ear, their beautiful suits were beginning to take the bashing the life of a Big A man had to accept. They shook themselves and then went racing out of the smashed doorway and down the stairs.

They leaped down the steps and started around the corner for the alley.

The old Cortina bellowed as Quinn gunned her.

The car flew out of the alley mouth scattering Bodie and Doyle like paper cups abandoned after a soccer match.

They flattened themselves away against the sides and the Cortina flashed past. Quinn looked extraordinarily big and authoritative behind the wheel. They did not forget he had an assault rifle in there with him.

They ran back to the Capri.

Doyle grabbed the R/T.

'4.5 to Base. Patch me through to Alpha.'

In the Cortina Quinn wrestled with the wheel to bring the car sliding around a corner. A white car was in pursuit, and it didn't matter who was driving that car, he or she was bad news for Quinn. He had to shake the white car - fast!

He came out of that skidding turn to crunch his side against a parked car. Bits of metal flew. The Cortina snaked. Quinn fought the wheel, held her on line, stamped his foot down and sent her howling down the centre of the road.

The car he'd hit looked sad, a side dented in and windows smashed.

As the owner of that sad car raced up, raving, the Capri hit the corner in a controlled skid. Bodie held her beautifully, drifting around, catching her and then hitting the throttle as she lined up. The Capri bellowed with power, pounced after the Cortina.

The chase continued.

Good though Quinn was he was never going to shake a Capri with the quality of driver pursuing him. Quinn was very good, as George Cowley was at pains to point out; but, then, so were Doyle and Bodie . . .

Sometimes, George Cowley didn't really realise just how good, when they put their minds to it, Bodie and Doyle were. Trouble was, they had lapses . . .

Now Bodie closed the gap remorselessly. Despite all Quinn's twists and turns, Bodie held him. They sizzled round a corner and Quinn glimpsed his salvation. In the busy streets this familiar situation was bound to occur once in a while . . .

The clumsy lorry backing out from a narrow high-gated entrance half-blocked the street. A man stood by the tailgate waving his arms. He might not have existed as far as Quinn was concerned.

The Cortina hissed between the parked car to the left and the tailgate to the right. The man waving his arms spun around like a top. The truck inched back another foot.

Bodie saw all that, saw the size of the gap, and slammed on the anchors. The Capri slewed, rubber smoking, ended up broadside on and rubbing doorsills with the truck.

Doyle leaned out of the open window and yelled. He had to do that. His curly hair looked like a bunch of electric wires, the marks on his face vivid with passion. But, even as he yelled, he and Bodie knew it was no go . . .

'Get that out of here!' Doyle made shooshing movements.

By the time they'd got through and reached the first T-junction, that fifty-percent chance went right down at the next. They'd had him and they'd lost him.

They were not altogether happy about the reception Cowley would accord them. They reported back to him at the bedsit and found Cowley poking around. Doyle opened the batting by saying: 'We fell for the oldest trick in the book.'

Cowley said: 'I'm not surprised. Quinn saw the first edition.'

Bodie looked at the list of black-scrawled names on the wall.

'Interesting list . . .'

'With,' Doyle pointed out unnecessarily. 'Granger crossed off.'

'Do you know who they are, sir?'

Cowley nodded and half-turned away. 'Yes. They're the men who formed the chain of command when Quinn was sent to bring out the defector.'

'And now,' said Bodie. 'It's a death list.'

Cowley looked at the floor and didn't answer that, so Doyle said: 'We'd better put them under protective surveillance – '

Cowley looked up. 'In Leniston's case that won't be necessary. He died a few months ago, natural causes.'

'Well, that leaves Howard and Morris as probable targets.'

'Howard's back with the army.' Cowley stared at the list of names. 'Bomb disposal. You'd better get over there.'

Doyle said: 'And Morris?'

George Cowley said: 'I'll take care of Morris.'

As his agents left, Cowley remained staring at the death list.

The ancient car rolled forward along the level concrete. It reached the lip of a muddy incline. There was no driver behind the wheel. The old banger tipped over the incline and began to roll steadily down.

With a rip of orange and a stab of dark smoke, the old car exploded. She blew apart. The bang cracked against the Capri as Bodie tooled it in and parked. The two CI5 men watched as the group of soldiers appeared from the protection of their safety wall. They picked up their man instantly.

When they reached the group, consisting of a couple of bomb disposal officers in uniform and Major Howard in civvies, Howard was finishing up his small lecture.

'On level ground the device was safe. As the car went down the incline the mercury in the switch ran forward and completed the detonation circuit.'

Bodie and Doyle whilst they walked towards Howard, also managed to take cognizance of their surroundings. The bomb-disposal training area looked as though it had been blown up and put back together again – and again . . .

'Major Howard?'

'Yes?' Howard's little frown was allayed as Doyle produced his I.D.

'We'd like to talk to you, sir.'

As Howard hesitated, Doyle glanced sideways at the soldiers, and Howard got the message right away. He nodded.

'Carry on, you two. See if you can identify the explosive.'

The two soldiers acknowledged the order and started off towards the wrecked car. Major Howard's little bomb had created comprehensive damage.

'Now,' said the major as he strolled with Bodie and Doyle towards the nearest of the single-storey buildings. 'What can I do for you?'

'An agent called Quinn,' began Bodie. 'Do you remember him?'

'Quinn.' Major Howard had no need to search his memory. 'Yes, a bad business. Ended up in Repton, didn't he?'

In his flat yet tripwire way, the touch of irony always there, Doyle said: 'He broke out.'

'We found your name on a possible assassination list.' Bodie's dryness was pronounced. They handled this like a one-two. Howard's face remained composed.

'I – see.'

'We,' said Doyle. 'Are here to offer you protective custody.'

'So you're taking the threat seriously?'

'Colonel Granger was shot this morning. He was the first name.'

Howard's face, although remaining as before, turned away. Howard said: 'And Quinn was responsible?'

'It looks that way.'

Doyle recited the list. 'Granger, yourself, Leniston, Morris.'

'You do know,' said Howard. 'Leniston's dead?'

Bodie nodded. 'Yes.'

They had reached the entrance to the building.

Howard paused. He hitched his neck inside his collar.

'So,' he said, his manner brisk, no nonsense. 'That leaves myself and George Cowley.'

For a very short time, it didn't sink in. It didn't sink in fast enough to stop Doyle from repeating: 'George Cowley?'

'Yes.' Howard missed the surprise. 'Morris was his nickname. Morris Cowley, the old pre-war car.' He turned to go into the building. 'George was always known as Morris in the old days.'

Major Howard went inside out of the sunshine.

Bodie and Doyle looked, one at the other, and they did not like at all, not one slightest little bit, what they had just learned.

A killing machine called Quinn was on the loose with a rifle . . .

And George Cowley was on his death list . . .

Chapter Three

Quinn dropped the assault rifle off the top of the wall. He dropped it carefully and with precision onto a patch of soft ground. Then he jumped down and scooped it up. Mistreating equipment was anathema to anyone with sensibilities. The bomb disposal place was much as it had been. He looked around, then loped off to get into the cover of the explosive's building.

He reached the white-washed brick wall and eased along, back flat, ready to take a peep around the corner. The place, after the bangs of earlier, was now comfortably quiet.

If there were to be any more bangs, Quinn would be the man to make them.

He reached the corner and took his recce look. Just as he did so one of the soldiers came out of the doorway. He'd no doubt been checking on the type of explosive used.

The soldier bent. Quinn heard the jangle of keys, and seized his chance.

He went in like that famous jungle hunting cat, but Quinn was cold and deadly, racing in to knock the soldier out and as he fell to bundle his unconscious body back inside the building. Quinn moved fast. He stepped over the soldier, on into the explosives building, and then dragged the man inside.

After that Quinn was on the prowl, with an assault rifle, and a death list in his brain.

Bodie emerged from the entrance to the main building block first. Doyle followed and then Major Howard, who had donned a bulky British Warm. Quinn spotted the group almost at once. He saw the white Capri, he saw the distance they'd have to go to reach it, and the computations took no time at all.

He dropped onto his back taking a single magazine from his pocket. With the rifle above him he slapped the magazine in and then rolled onto his belly. The rifle snouted. Quinn peered through the scope. It was all very smooth, very professional, very deadly.

Quinn took deliberate aim.

Bodie reached the car and opened the door for Howard.

Quinn centred the cross hairs on Howard.

Howard started for the open door.

Quinn pressed the trigger.

The assault rifle let rip with its own brand of bang, and Howard jerked, slammed against the side of the car. Doyle raced in, grabbed Howard and dragged him down. Bodie's .41 Magnum whipped out in a fast draw. He took cover by the boot, trying to spot the gunman.

He called across to Doyle, using the old Bodie side-of-the-mouth communications technique.

'Howard all right?'

Doyle looked down at the major. He pulled the British Warm aside. Beneath lay a B.C.F. Fifty Nine jacket, a garment manufactured of criss-crossing layers of carbon fibre, quite thin, that was one of the latest bullet-proof jackets around. Doyle rummaged beneath the BCF59 and pulled the shirt away. Howard's chest would be bruised; but he was sound otherwise.

'He's badly shaken; but all right.' And, to Howard: 'Stay down. Play dead.'

A couple of soldiers ran out of the building, looking alarmed. Bodie bellowed.

'Get back! Keep clear!'

They backed off. They recongised the tone of voice.

Quinn stared at his rifle, and at the car. He could not see anyone now. But those two men would be – yes, there they were. Two men, each taking a flank, creeping out from the car. They were out to shoot him. Quinn got to his knee and loosed off a pitter-patter of shots, then climbed to his feet and ran.

Bodie and Doyle stood up and chased after him.

Running, Quinn realised in his confusion that he wouldn't reach the wall before his pursuers were on him. And, as he ran, his confusion tangled with his thoughts – they were not K.G.B. after him now. He could hear no baying of dogs slavering to sink their fangs into him. There was a list, and he had to do something about the list; but first he had to get away . . .

He saw the explosives store and pelted towards the door.

He halted in the doorway and turned, taking deliberate aim. He got off one shot and then the mag was empty and the rifle clicked dry. Bodie and Doyle threw themselves sideways and hit the dirt.

In the explosives store Quinn, with a rifle and no ammunition for it, looked about desperately. The shelves were loaded with munitions; but there would be no ammunition for this brand of assault rifle . . .

He selected grenades and smoke grenades, stuffing his pockets.

Bodie and Doyle advanced on the building. Quinn had not shot again.

Doyle yelled.

'Come out, Quinn!'

There was no answer. Only the sunlight laying butter-yellow slabs against the explosive's store, and the big black gap of the doorway. Bodie and Doyle looked at the black rectangle, then at each other, and then at the doorway.

This was the sort of thing they were paid to do. It was a part of their job. Doing it more than once didn't make it any the easier. It was never a simple get-on-with-it routine chore. Each time they could wind up dead or mutilated.

Each man took a breath, braced himself, got set.

Together, they rushed the door.

They burst in, out of the sunlight, and froze.

Quinn held a grenade in his hand.

He gripped the pin between his teeth. Deliberately, the big man spat out the pin. He took a step forward.

He went to the doorway, past Bodie and Doyle who had, quite correctly, hurled themselves to the sides out of the direct line of fire. There was nothing they could do. Quinn stalked past. At the doorway tension crackled like electricity in the store.

If he tossed that grenade now . . .

With a movement at once deliberate and taunting, Quinn let the lever move by a fraction . . .

Bodie and Doyle remained frozen.

Quinn clamped the lever shut, turned, and sprinted away across the open ground.

The two CI5 men hauled their feet off the floor, for to both of them it felt as though they stood in a lake of treacle. They ran out after Quinn. He was just vanishing around the back of the main buildings.

The partners ran for the end building where Quinn had darted out of sight. Abruptly he reappeared. It was all very quick. He threw the grenade.

They saw it coming and dived away, rolling into the wall.

The grenade went off with a splendid bang; even if the bang was small beer beside the real bangs that denotated around here. Even whilst the noise hung on the air and the smoke wafted, Bodie and Doyle sprang to their feet and raced for the opening between the main buildings and the sheds at their back.

The two lines of construction formed a narrow alley.

Quinn sprinted along at the far end.

As Bodie and Doyle appeared and chased along between the buildings, Quinn turned and hurled a smoke grenade.

The thing plopped. Great gouts and gobbets of smoke billowed.

Choking in the smoke, blinded, reeling, Bodie and Doyle staggered along to the far end. By the time their smarting eyes could take in the bomb disposal training area without it being obscured by waterfalls, Quinn had gone.

A little later the military pick-up truck which would take Major Howard to a place of safety pulled up before the main buildings. The red-tape had been cleared. The bomb-disposal training area now looked as peaceful as it ever would look. Howard walked out of the building flanked by Bodie and Doyle.

'You should be safe now,' said Doyle. 'As far as Quinn's concerned - you're dead.'

Howard put his hand on the door handle.

'And Morris. What about Morris?' Cowley -'

Doyle and Bodie had no ready answer to that. They watched as Howard climbed into the truck and was immediately driven away. When he'd gone, Bodie and Doyle looked about, and if they were expecting to see Quinn or expecting to see Cowley was not clear from their expressions.

Doyle summed up their feelings.

'Cowley! Alias Morris, alias devious, double-dealing, two-faced b – '

Bodie interrupted.

'Let's go.'

They tracked Cowley through a call to control and they homed in on Cowley's car as the old man made for it, stomping across the pavement. He walked with his limp, sturdily, and he acted as though he had the city to himself and there was no killing machine with an assault rifle and a list of names written in blacking on a wall . . .

The sun was beginning to decline. Bodie and Doyle had had time to pick up a sandwich; but they both knew there was no time for eating. Not when Morris Cowley was poised at the wrong end of a rifle barrel.

Doyle abruptly appeared as Cowley reached for the door handle of his Rover. Cowley twisted to stare.

'Allow me,' said Doyle. 'Morris.'

Cowley straightened as Doyle opened the door. He stared at Doyle, and then at Bodie, standing with his partner. One thing you had to say, Cowley kept his composure superbly. He just bashed on as though nothing had changed. Well, for him, probably nothing had.

'What's the situation on Major Howard?'

'Quinn made a try,' Bodie told him. 'But he's safe.'

'Now,' said Doyle, and his words carried almost as much meaning as his tone. 'All we've got to do is take care of you.'

'Where's your car?'

'Right behind you, sir.'

Again Doyle's tone and words conveyed the fact that that was where the Capri was going to be from now on. Glued to the exhaust pipe of Cowley's Rover. Cowley hunched up his shoulder, and then got into his car. The partners could see he wasn't at all pleased with the situation. The two cars pulled away in convoy.

Cowley looked back through the rear window. The white car hung on close behind. Cowley said, half to himself, half to his driver: 'I suppose there isn't a chance ... No.' He shook his head. He knew Bodie and Bodie's driving skills. 'No, forget it.'

Things had been arranged and in the Capri Bodie checked with Doyle.

'What about the safe house?'

'All taken care of. There'll be a man on every entrance, one on the roof, another on the building opposite.' Doyle had been busy on the R/T as Bodie drove. 'Three patrolling the streets outside.'

'Good. Well, that's where the boss sleeps tonight.'

'He'll have to sleep rough.'

'Why?'

Doyle's lilt of laughter was most pronounced.

'There's only a camp bed.'

Bodie shook his sleek head. 'He's not going to like that.' Bodie sounded as though he liked it, though.

The safe house was reached in good order, situated in a quiet side street it slumbered away beyond shrubbery and trees, unassuming, suburban, unremarkable. That it housed men quick with guns would have been regarded as incredible, impossible, by the residents of the street.

The room Cowley surveyed was simply furnished, with a low coffee table, a camp bed in a corner, a chair. He sat on the sofa and pointed intemperately at the coffee table.

'This is too low. I intend to work.'

Doyle watched as Cowley stood, strode to the window.

'And,' said Cowley. 'I'll need more light.'

He marched across to the camp bed and thumped it.

'Well,' said the chief of CI5, 'at least, the bed is adequate.'

Bodie's eyes went up to heaven. The only thing the old man liked was the bed.

Quinn eased into the bookshop without any fuss.

An eerie quality lay in this musty repository of learning, the windows shafted a dim moonlight that emphasised cobwebs that were not really there, and quill pens and whispers. The shadowy figure of Quinn passed between ranked stacks of learning and enjoyment and started to pad up the stairs. He reached the half-landing leading to the living quarters. The sound of a running shower reached him from the shower room to the side, built into a partitioned room. He hesitated.

Across the glass panel door the light spilled out, silhouetting the naked figure of a woman leaving the shower room, reaching for the handle of the door. Quinn froze. Then he pulled back out of the room into the shadows of the half landing.

The door opened a fraction. Teresa Quinn's voice called: 'Jack! Don't go to sleep. Bring me another glass. There's a bottle in the fridge.'

The shape of the woman beyond the glass stirred memories for Quinn, memories he did not wish disturbed. Jack . . . ? He backed away, feeling behind him with open hands, his face reflecting pain. Fate struck him blows he could not understand. This was just another body blow . . .

Silently, a man called Quinn padded away, and anguish tore at the core of the killing machine.

Outside the chief's door in the safe house Bodie stood guard. He did not feel in the slightest ridiculous or superfluous. Allison was running the outside team, and there were good men surrounding the chief. Doyle walked along the little corridor from the kitchen with a folder tucked under his arm and a mug of tea in his other hand.

Bodie smiled his crinkled lip smile.

'Bring me one?'

Doyle's answering smile was all Doyle, not quite sly, not quite mischievous, but damn near!

'Officers only.'

Bodie sniffed and looked pained.

'Thanks a lot . . .'

Doyle knocked and entered.

Cowley sat up on the camp bed as Doyle came in. He saw the mug of tea and the folder. A trestle table had been brought into the room. Cowley brightened, his fair hair ruffled, making him look like an angry rooster.

'Cup of tea, sir.'

'Thanks.' He swung his legs to the floor and nodded at the file. 'That the pathologist's report?'

'Yes, sir.'

Taking the file, Cowley crossed to the trestle table, which was already beginning to accumulate its quota of papers, and riffled the file out. He found what he wanted. He pulled out a blow-up of the photomicrograph of the bullet that had killed Granger and compared it with the blow-up of another bullet from another file.

'The bullet that killed Granger,' said Cowley, tapping the new photo, 'and the bullet that missed me.'

Doyle knew about forensics when it came to ballistics. So did Cowley. Both men saw at once that the bullets, although of the same calibre, had been fired from different rifles.

'Two guns,' said Doyle. '*Two* gunmen ...'

'I think we're making progress,' said Cowley in his most plummy way. 'Thank you, Doyle.'

Recognising this as a dismissal, Doyle left the chief to his tea and his cogitations. Two rifles, then ...

He checked with Bodie and went off to make sure all the men were still at their stations.

Dawn was soon due, and Doyle's eyelids felt as though they'd been sandpapered and hung out to dry in the Sahara. When he checked with Cook, on the stairs, Cook was chirpy enough.

'All clear here, Ray.'

'Check.' As Doyle went to pass, Cook added: 'Makes a change from the routine obbo caper, this.'

'Oh?'

'Been keeping an obbo on a house over towards Pentonville way for a fortnight now. Nothing doing there, if you ask me. June's right fed up.'

'Haven't seen June in some time. How's the - ?'

'Going to be a boy. Dead cert.'

Luck, Cookie,' said Doyle, and called out the rest of the squad on his R/T.

'Rear entrance?'

'Clear,' said his R/T.

'Roof A?'

'Nothing to report.' That was Alan Jones, a regular driver for the Big A.

'Roof B?'

Nothing on the handset.

Doyle repeated: 'Roof B. Come in, Roof B.'

Roof B was Jimmy Coourtney. Doyle headed for the stairs, fast. Again he tried and again received no answer.

Racing up the stairs, Doyle shouted the alarm into his handset.

'Possible intruder . . . Opposite roof . . .'

Bodie picked that up instantly and cracked open the door to the chief's room without ceremony.

Cowley was studying the photographs again and he looked up, his glasses perched, as Bodie burst in.

'We might have flushed him out!'

Cowley grabbed for his jacket. If there was action, the chief of the Big A wouldn't be left out.

Doyle reached the roof, flung open the slanted door, and scrambled out. A CI5 man on patrol was carefully scanning his area with night glasses.

'See anything, Alan?'

'Nothing.'

Doyle grabbed the night glasses and doubled around the edge of the roof, perilously close to the parapet. He looked off towards the opposite roof. Despite his exertions and the fact his hair was a mere mop of bristled curls, the night glasses in Doyle's hands were rock steady.

Bodie's voice floated from the R/T.

'4.5. What have you got?'

Doyle scanned the opposite building's roof.

At that moment Quinn, on the roof, was finishing up the neat but not gaudy task of fixing a cup-discharger and grenade to the rifle. The unconscious body of Jimmy Coourtney lay to one side, his R/T spilled from one lax hand.

Quinn set the grenade launcher and then slanted the rifle. He could hit a gnat's eye with this, at this range, and the target window was big enough for a swarm of gnats.

Desperately panning the glasses, Doyle, saw that movement swim into his field of vision. He saw the hunched shape, the rifle, the bulbous attachment . . .

He grabbed his R/T up, yelling like a maniac.

'Bodie! Get the old man out of there! *Fast*!'

Quinn fired the grenade.

Bodie got the call and didn't wait to wonder what the hell was going on. He just grabbed Cowley, tangled up in his coat, and fairly hurled him out of the door. Both men skidded into the corridor and tumbled sideways as the room and the door filled with flame and smoke and a crashing concussion smashed about their ears. The corridor choked up with smoke and bits of plaster fell off the ceiling. Both men looked like flour-millers after a night out at the sweep's beano.

Bodie pulled himself up. His famous lips crinkled. Fastidiously, he started to brush himself off. He looked at the chief. He spoke very solicitously.

'Had you finished your tea, sir?'

Cowley took a piece of plaster from his hair.

'No. Some idiot put sugar in it.'

'Tut,' said Bodie, 'tut.'

And, with that, Cowley stalked off.

Bodie gazed after him, shaking his head.

'It'll probably go down in Doyle's file.' He spoke reprovingly. 'Sugar in the tea ...'

Washed, shaved, changed, bright and shining, George Cowley sat in the back of the white Capri as Bodie tooled the car along in the early morning sunshine. Doyle sat next to him. They both looked beat, their once-immaculate clothes more than the worse for wear.

In his best voice, Cowley said: 'You must be tired. Why don't you two go and get some sleep?'

'We,' said Bodie. 'Are fine.'

'We,' said Doyle. 'Are going to stick to you – '

'Like,' finished Bodie. 'Glue.' Then, after a pause, he added: 'Sir.'

Cowley peered over his heavy glasses.

'Very commendable.'

By contrast to the dryness in his words the Gobi desert must have been a watersports marina.

He glanced out of the window as they passed a parade of shops leading up to a departmental store. The sunshine brisked up the paving stones, and the shop fronts shone.

'Pull over. I want to buy some – ' a slight pause. Then: 'Toothpaste.'

Bodie pulled the car over, finding no difficulty in parking this early, and Cowley got out. 'I won't be a minute.'

The partners watched the chief enter the little shop with the advertising obscuring most of the windows, and then come out and walk up the street towards the department store.

'Where's he going now?' demanded Doyle. 'That place has a dozen exists.'

'At least.'

'The stupid, pig-headed old goat!' fumed Doyle. 'If we don't watch it we'll lose him.' He started to get out of the car.

Bodie hauled him back.

'Maybe not.'

The look on Bodie's face, with that incurving nostril and crinkle to the lips was one of the utmost smugness. He held out a miniature radio receiver that emitted a tinny bleep.

Doyle opened his mouth. He turned his head half-sideways as he said with that incredulous laugh in his voice: 'You bugged George Cowley?'

'Why not,' said Bodie. 'He's bugged me often enough.'

Cowley found no difficulty in shaking the well-intentioned shadowing efforts of his two top agents. He made his way via public transport – which was something to make him smile, relishing the joke – to the country cottage, now uninhabited and overgrown. He stood for a moment beneath the drooping FOR SALE sign, staring around. The country was friendly, around here, narrow lanes and orchards and quietness. All the same, they'd had some rare old shindigs here, setting up missions, organising, training, preparing themselves mentally for the challenges ahead.

He walked into the overgrown garden and waited by the twisted tree, large and sere, just past the straggling roses.

Cowley heard the movement to his rear. He didn't know if he was first or if Quinn was first.

He said: 'That you, laddie?'

Quinn's voice reached him, flat and somehow hollow, dead. 'Don't turn around, Morris.'

'Leniston's dead.' Cowley did not turn around, not just yet. There were things to be said first. 'I thought you'd come. Leniston wouldn't be happy to see his garden in this state.'

Quinn stepped out from the shelter of the tree. He raised the rifle slowly, lifting it until it pointed at Cowley's back, between the shoulder blades. Quinn's finger rested on the trigger.

As though the rifle could extend an invisible finger of force, and penetrate Cowley's heart, he knew the muzzle was centred directly on him. He spoke slowly, quietly, with a soothing tone.

'Remember the pub down the road. Those drunken evenings ... Staggering back up here to sleep it off ...'

Quinn began to shake. The shakes started slowly at first, but increased as Cowley went on speaking. Quinn could remember. As though the process he had gone through could trigger other things than lists scrawled in blacking on a wall ... He flopped sideways to lean against the tree. The rifle fell from his hands.

'I remember being ditched.' Quinn's voice came hoarsely. His face contorted. He was sweating. 'I remember being tortured – '

'Yes,' said Cowley, and his voice held infinite pity. 'Yes. I know what they did to you.'

Cowley could hear Quinn groaning at the other side of the tree. He began to turn around.

'I told you not to turn around.' Quinn's voice rapped out, hard, a temporary return to his other self.

'All right. But listen to me. I want to put something to you –'

'It's too late – '

'They handed you over to the K.G.B. You were tough, trained to resist; but they worked on you. They programmed you to kill. They gave you the names, planted them deep in your subconscious – '

Quinn shuddered. He wiped his mouth, drooling.

'They wouldn't let me sleep – '

Cowley went on mercilessly, yet filled with compassion.

'Granger. Howard. Leniston – and Morris.'

Quinn couldn't see the garden, couldn't see Cowley. He stared back into horror.

'They attached electrodes to my temples. I remember the wires, red and green. Those damned wires ...'

'Then you were exchanged. You came home. What happened?'

Quinn did not answer. His breathing disturbed the silence with its gasping sucking in of air, its jagged exhalations.

'You fought the programming, didn't you, laddie. You managed finally to – reject it. But the cost was too high.' This explained Quinn's actions, this pathetic tale explained why Quinn had become as he had. It did not give the answers Cowley wanted. 'That cost was mental collapse. Yet, two days ago at the clinic, the trigger was re-set.'

Whilst Cowley was as well aware as anyone that he was handling what amounted to a fused stick of dynamite with the fuse burning, he knew that he had to go on. Here lay the clue, the answer to what triggered Quinn, the deaths of good men, the stirring of purpose in a disoriented mind.

Something Cowley said registered with Quinn. His big open face screwed up with the effort of remembering. He did know, he could work it through ... Through the lights and the voices of the interrogators and the high-collared uniforms and the vicious dogs, through the gates and walls, through the needles and the injections ...

Quinn said: 'The trigger was Krasnov.'

Now Cowley was jolted. He was surprised. The word came out almost before he was aware. 'Krasnov?'

'He was – was in the room.' Quinn faltered now, the clouds gathering, the clarity vanishing. 'Doctor Grey's room. He picked ... up ... the needle ...'

Through the clouds the face of Krasnov in his fake doctor's coat leered on Quinn, he could feel the grip on his arm and the needle going in, being forced in, and his futile struggles ...'

Cowley thought flat out, and then said, very carefully: 'We can turn it right around. It can work. But I'll need your help. Together we can pull it off. What do you say?'

Cowley heard no response from Quinn.

He went on: 'You can lead Krasnov into a trap. Remember the airfield, laddie?'

Again there was no answer. Slowly, Cowley began to turn around. He turned steadily, stoically, like a grenadier turning from column to square to receive a charge of cavalry.

Quinn was gone.

Cowley turned back swiftly the other way and there came the two prize partners, Bodie and Doyle, walking along the garden grass and smirking all over their ugly faces. Cowley favoured them with two malevolent looks that said, quite clearly: 'Well, I might have known!'

He said: 'You heard?'

'Most of it,' said Bodie. And Doyle added: 'Want us to follow him?'

Cowley shook his head. 'No. He's our link.'

He looked at his two top agents. His mouth pursed up. He looked like George Cowley looking like George Cowley. No one else could quite fashion that pursing, perusing, postulating broody stare. He thought he knew these two. Hell's bells and buckets of blood! He *did* know 'em! And a penny to a pinch of snuff it was Bodie. Just Bodie's style, unrepentant mercenary ...

'All right, Bodie. Where is it?'

Bodie looked perfectly surprised. His eyebrows took off.

'Don't play games!' Cowley sounded fierce. 'The homing device.'

Bodie looked abashed. A small boy, caught scrumping, he spoke meekly. 'Er – the lapel. Left lapel.'

Cowley flipped his left lapel aside and unpinned the bug. He handed it to Bodie like the surgeon hands the growth he's just cut out to the furnace attendant.

Then he brisked these two up with work.

'Yuri Krasnov. K.G.B. assassin. Responsible for at least a dozen killings all over the world.' Cowley had it all now. 'A good plan. You have to hand 'em that. Quinn was phased out, strictly a no-no. So trigger him, or at least pump him full of something that makes it appear he's reactivated. Then simply follow him.'

'Krasnov does the killing,' said Doyle. 'Quinn takes the blame.'

'Precisely. And, for our get-out, Quinn, of course, is the key.'

Bodie looked as though he was about to become agitated. 'You can't rely on him. He's unbalanced at best – at worst – '

'I believe I got through to him.'

Doyle looked as though he wasn't convinced, not convinced at all, about that claim.

'You're going to set yourself up,' he said, 'meet Quinn again knowing Krasnov will be close?'

'It's the only way. And this time I do it alone. Is that understood?'

With that Cowley turned and stalked off. He'd called for his car and Paula would be waiting. As he went Doyle put out a hand, looking highly agitated, about to stop him.

Bodie pulled his partner back.

'Let him go.'

'What?'

Cowley vanished out of the garden. Bodie showed Doyle the little radio-receiver that they'd used to track the bug on Cowley.

Bodie smirked.

'I double bugged him . . .'

A lifetime ago the Lancs used to trundle across the apron and line up and take turns to lift off and away into the growing night. Four Merlins thundering, hauling them along, props spinning, they'd ghost up and away and vanish into the evening. Some would come back, not all. They'd touch down with holes punched in wing or fuselage, an engine out, a heap of red goo in a tail turret. The crews would stumble out, shaking, and traipse off for de-briefing. There had been noise in the thunder of engines, the stink of oil and petrol and fumes, the memory of swing music, the horrors of flak-filled skies.

Later there had been a small private aircraft, and men dedicated to another war, and another way of waging their struggle . . .

Cowley was waiting. He stood in the crumbling doorway of the ops tower, half-shielded by the rusted ladder to the Lewis-gun site on the roof, waiting and watching.

The battered Cortina turned onto the airstrip. Quinn drove. He could barely see. In his tortured head voices rang and clamoured, each demanding to be heard over the others.

The male nurse taking the axe: 'You're wanted, Quinn. Doctor Grey . . . '

The First Interrogator: 'Why do you resist? Why do you fight it? You know we'll break you sooner or later . . . '

The Second Interrogator: 'Do you imagine your people in London are at all concerned about you now?'

And the First Interrogator again, insistent beyond the splay of light: 'Be sensible Quinn! They sent you knowing the risk . . . '

Another voice, plummy, rich, the voice of a man who had been a friend: 'They programmed you to kill . . . '

The First Interrogator: 'They sent you because to them you are expendable . . . '

Cowley again: 'Two days ago at the Clinic the trigger was re-set . . . '

'Why do you resist? Why do you fight it?'

And, George Cowley, finally: 'We can turn it right around. You can lead Krasnov into a trap . . . You can lead Krasnov into a trap . . . '

Quinn brought his car along the overgrown strip and turned. There was a clear run towards a brick communications hut in the distance. He got out of the car clasping the rifle and began to move towards the ops building. As he moved a sound of whirring buzzing fluttered up. He whirled, the rifle snouting.

A couple of pigeons, startled, flew up on whirring wings. Quinn tilted his head back and watched them fly. He saw their wings, and into his jumbled mind the sounds of his light aircraft broke, the spluttering cough of the engine as he gunned it along the runway for takeoff. Takeoff . . .

Cowley called: 'Over here.'

Quinn snapped out of the memory. He loped over to the ops building. He saw the Chief of CI5.

'Where's Krasnov?' Cowley remained perfectly calm.

'Here.' Quinn no longer mumbled. 'Somewhere.'

'This is where it all started. This is where we can finish it.'

The pause lengthened. The rifle twitched. Then Quinn nodded. That nod was agreement. Cowley let his breath out, drew his own automatic, and, together, the men moved out.

Working as a team they began to check out the decrepit buildings on the airfield. Working as a team – that brought the old memories flooding back!

The hangars lofted, tall and gaunt and decayed. The smaller buildings had sharp-angled corners, and behind any of those corners Krasnov could be waiting for them with a bullet each. Or, just to make sure, a whole stream of bullets pumped from an S.M.G. Quinn stayed back, rifle crouched, as Cowley led around the next corner. A shot cracked into the wall less than a foot from Cowley's bent head. Instantly, he dropped flat, auto snouting.

Lying in cover, Cowley glanced back at Quinn. The big man was alert, poised, searching. Across the angle of the hangar side a glimpse of movement? Quinn did not hesitate. He let off a Johnny-get-your-gun burst.

In the hangar and ducking back from the window, the man who had begun all this, calling himself Doctor Grey, the man who was a top assassin, Yuri Krasnov, just avoided Quinn's hose of lead. He grimaced. He flattened back against the wall.

Quinn took his right hand from the rifle, balancing it easily with his left, waved Cowley on. The chief of CI5 knew when to trust a man in action; he lifted to his feet and, bent double, scuttled for the far wall. Both men crouched beside the hangar wall. Now they guessed their quarry was inside. Purposefully, they made for the entrance, ready to flush him out.

Just inside the cavernous entrance, with the sunlight barred away, they checked their weapons. They glanced up, and their faces reflected their thoughts as their glances locked.

Cowley said: 'Ready?'

'Ready.'

They ran forward, spraying lead up into Krasnov's position by the window as they ran.

The assassin attempted to duck away. Bullets spat about him. One struck his hand and with a curse he dropped his gun. The weapon clattered down to the concrete floor.

In a strong compelling voice, Cowley called up.

'Come down, Krasnov.'

The sneer in Krasnov's tones was perfectly genuine.

'You don't think I'd be so foolish as to come here alone.'

Standing on the concrete, Cowley felt the breeze on his spine. But Quinn, half-turned, saw the other assassin first. The man, dressed in dark workmanlike clothes, held a gun aimed at Cowley's back. Without a second's hesitation, as the man fired, Quinn hurled himself forward. He seized Cowley around the waist and using all his big bulk drove them both away and into the cover of a pile of crates.

But Quinn took the bullet meant for George Cowley.

The assault rifle lay on the concrete beyond the crates, out of reach. Quinn held his shoulder, and blood seeped onto his fingers. More bullets lashed around the untidy huddle of crates. Cowley, unhurt, stared about. There was no way out of the crossfire, and now there were three gunmen besides the chief assassin shooting at them. Methodically, Cowley reloaded his auto. This was a sticky one . . .

With a screeching whine the white Capri erupted onto the airfield, slewed to a wild stop in a stink of burning rubber. Doyle heard the shots.

'The hangar.'

Bodie span the wheel, gunned the car, sent it roaring for the wide hangar doors.

The car went burning into the shadows of the hangar.

One gunman, caught for the moment in the open, yelped and tried to jump clear. Bodie, his lips thinned, went into a sliding skid. The Capri howled broadside on and smashed into the gunman. He was swept away like a rag doll. The car halted shuddering.

Leaping out, revolvers in their fists, Bodie and Doyle hit the concrete and rolled away from the fire of the second and third gunmen, who shot flurriedly, switching their aim from the pile of crates.

The two gunmen were incautious. Or maybe they were overconfident. Bodie half-lifted and brought his revolver up. He shot just the once. The big slug took the K.G.B. man and knocked him away even as Bodie yelled: 'Behind you!'

Doyle whirled.

The third gunman closed in, aiming to hit Doyle. Ray

Doyle - champion marksman on the force - cut loose and the gunman span away, dropping his weapon, screeching.

Left alone, Krasnov made a run for it.

In the confusion of the skidding car, the screams of wounded men, the shattering crash of gunfire in the echoing vault of the hangar, he pelted past, heading for the doors and freedom.

Cowley spotted the running figure of Krasnov. Doyle saw him, too, and started to follow, revolver lifted.

Cowley said: 'He's mine.'

He stepped forward from the crates, picked up Quinn's assault rifle. Bodie and Doyle, respecting what the chief was doing, watched. Krasnov ran fleetly, away from the hangar, out over the apron, haring like a maniac for his car.

It would not be an easy shot.

Grim-faced, carefully, Cowley took his aim.

He centred the cross hairs. He led the target, and then, exquisitely, pressed the trigger.

Krasnov threw up his arms and fell.

Bodie shook his head. Doyle holstered his weapon. They stepped up to stand beside their chief.

For a moment the silence stretched.

They stared out into the sunshine at the small crumpled form, a dark blot, still and unmoving.

Then Cowley looked about.

'Quinn. Where is he?'

This was the airfield from which Quinn's last great adventure had begun, the mission that had gone disastrously wrong for him. His brain had been tampered with. His mind broken. The drugs had triggered a species of semi-autonomous action. The wound in his shoulder bit in. He was losing blood. Fantasies crowded Quinn's mind, memories mingling and reverberating. He staggered towards his car, clutching his shoulder, lurching along. He was going out to the aeroplane. He would pilot himself, safer that way, fly out and do the job and liberate the defector and fly home.

Granger's voice hammered at him in memory: 'The mission is of vital importance, Quinn.' He stumbled on over the concrete. 'You take off at 0600 hours.'

He climbed into the car and started up. In his head he heard the splutter of the plane engine, was taxying ready for takeoff.

Cowley saw the car moving and yelled to Bodie.

'Get the car.'

For Quinn the takeoff was now the most important object in all the world. He rolled faster and faster.

Control came in. 'This is control. You are clear for take-off.'

'Roger control.' Quinn spoke in the clipped accents of navigational communication. The plane gathered speed . . .

Bodie gunned the Capri after the racing Cortina.

Quinn checked his instruments. Control came on again, hissing into Quinn's mind. 'Wind speed six knots. Cloud ceiling four thousand.'

Now the two cars were neck and neck, screaming along the runway. Dust whipped back in a lifting plume, mingled and mixed, writhing after them.

Tensely, Doyle said: 'He's running out of runway.'

Cowley gripped his fists. 'Brake, Quinn.' He spoke aloud, uselessly. 'Brake!'

Quinn sat relaxed, perfectly calm. He sat in the cockpit of a light aeroplane, taking off for a hazardous mission. Perhaps, in those final moments, the truth revealed itself. He sat in an old Cortina, roaring along a runway, and he had no wings to lift him up, up and up, soaring away into the blue . . .

Bodie hit the brakes and the Capri slewed to a skating halt. The Cortina went straight on. It hit the rough ground at the end of the runway, bounced straight on into the brick communications hut. Smashed in the impact, the car looked like a squashed insect for just long enough for Cowley to leap out and start running . . .

The car exploded.

The petrol tank went up in a ball of flame.

In that billowing inferno of fire and smoke, the CI5 men were driven back, arms over their faces. They watched. For Bodie and Doyle there was nothing to say. For Cowley . . .

'Fly free,' said George Cowley. 'Fly free, laddie.'

Perhaps a man called Quinn had found his wings.

Chapter Four

As a very smart brief whose reputation with the police was perhaps not as high as it might be, Hockley regarded himself as remarkably successful in his chosen profession. He ran a flashy Porsche. His flat was elegant, discreet and obviously expensive. And, with it all, he was a suave young solicitor who had ways and means of charming his clients.

In the current case, a young tearaway had turned Queen's Evidence in the middle of a trial. There were political implications; but there was also money, a great deal of money, in the background. This Jimmy Kilpin needed careful handling.

Kilpin wore his own clothes as he was still on trial. He was clearly extremely nervous all during the interview in the remand prison. And yet Hockley handled him without too much concern, without much of the velvet glove.

'I talked this morning with Sir George – '

Kilpin interrupted eagerly.

'What's he say?'

Hockley shook his head. 'He still thinks we need more.'

The desperation stood starkly in Jimmy Kilpin's voice. He worked himself into a frenzy, fighting the feeling of being in a hole with the earth being shovelled on top of him.

'I've told them everything I know! *Everything*! Facts . . . Names . . . Codes . . . '

'Oh, yes, Mr Kilpin, he's aware of that.' Hockley hesitated, deliberately, letting the acid work right into Kilpin's spirit. 'He thinks it'll be a nominal sentence – '

Jimmy Kilpin shuddered. 'I'll still have to do time?'

'An open prison.' Hockley kept up the pressure. 'Police supervision – they're good at these things.'

Kilpin put his hands to his head. 'Someone'll put a knife in me.' He was horrified by the prospect before him. 'You should see the way they look at me here. That so-called accident in the kitchen – '

Hockley sounded genuinely concerned. 'Yes. Sir George wondered if you knew anything about arms dumps, bomb repositories. Anything like that?'

'There's an arms dump in a field in Kent.'

Hockley looked as though he was pleased for Kilpin at last. 'There is? Could you find it?' As Kilpin nodded, he went on: 'Well, that's it, then. Might be the difference between five years and nothing. Don't mention my name – this is your idea, you must get the credit. Wait till I've been gone about an hour, then contact the Prison Governor. Tell him about it, he'll contact the Judge.'

'You think this could swing it?' Kilpin looked up.

Hockley smiled reassuringly, very smooth, very suave. 'I'd bet on it.' His smile lingered on Jimmy Kilpin.

That new Porsche of his took him swimmingly away from the remand prison. His first port of call was a public telephone box. He dialled out for the telephone box number he'd been given. His – associates – would be most interested.

Sitting on the old stone wall by the telephone box on the outskirts of the village, young Tree read his newspaper and kicked his heels. He had a sly look about him, had young Tree; but he was quick on his feet, with a sharp nose and eyes of a pale hue. The phone in the box rang and young Tree hopped off the wall to answer.

When he took the news in, he smiled, hung up on Hockley and took himself off back to the caravan site. Ulrike had found the place advertised in a shop window – on a grubby postcard – and they'd hired the two caravans for three weeks or so. It had been a clever move. Young Tree trudged back along the road, turned off onto an unmetalled path and so, cutting in under the edge of the orchard, and crossing a field, ducking under a rotting wooden fence, came to the caravan site. It was situated in a really charming spot, with orchards all about, and with hopgardens across the curve of the hill. The sky was tall and blue with a few fluffy clouds. It was the time of year for holidays – or would have been . . .

There were three of the comrades playing cards at a rickety old table. Hens clucked about, the wire netting of their coop hanging adrift. The ground was already tending to mud where they'd been trudging back and forth. The two caravans were water-tight, had curtains to the windows, and power and lights. A transistor radio pumped out hot music into the warm air; no-one was reading, and Ulrike was washing her hair.

A zinc bath stood on an apple box beside the entrance to her caravan. A towel draped around her neck as she bent her head, steadily soaping with the supermarket shampoo, then rinsing carefully. She was bare from the waist up; but the towel kept her decent. Anyway, no one was bothered about that for the moment; each one had a job to do.

When young Tree got back from the phone box Ulrike, with her senses alert, called: 'What did he say?'

Tree gave his thumbs up sign.

'It's on.'

Ulrike twisted the towel about her wet hair. She had a heavy, strong-boned face, with deep dimples beside her mouth. She looked what she was, a woman dedicated to an end in life, and not caring how she attained her goal. Now, she saw herself up there in lights, in black-headlines, known the world over, alongside Baader Meinhof, Carlos and the rest.

The routine observation up Pentonville way was quite clearly going to yield no results, and a few days later Cowley sent Bodie and Doyle to clear up shop. They found Cook sitting by the window, unshaven, a blanket over his shoulders, moodily looking at the remains of a sandwich. Field glasses, telephoto cameras, all the paraphernalia of an observation, cluttered the little room. The sound of church bells disturbed the silence.

'Anything happen at all?' said Bodie.

'Number Nineteen's growing cannabis in his window box.'

Bodie opened his eyes wide. 'Fact?'

'Either that,' said Cook, stretching and letting the blanket slip. 'Or petunias.'

Around Cook's neck hung a thin gold chain, with a medallion swinging against his throat. He started to clear up. 'I'm on Robbie Allison's caper,' he said.

'Haven't heard about that,' said Doyle. 'Last time we were all out together it was hairy – '

'Jim Coourtney was lucky –' Cook shook his head, remembering. 'We're collecting Jimmy Kilpin from the local nick.'

Bodie wrinkled his nostrils. 'Super Grass Junior!'

'Where you taking him?' said Doyle. 'Somewhere high, I hope.'

Cook shook his head. 'Nice idea. To dig up some guns, bombs, terrorists' stock-in-trade.'

'Who's going?'

'Allison, me, a couple of the lads. Transit van, picks, shovels, nut-crackers, whole shebang.'

Bodie looked at the tall blue sky through the window.

'Lovely day for it.'

Cook collected up the rest of his gear. He started for the door after some more typical Bodie and Doyle chitchat.

'Drop in some time, Ray. June often talks about you . . . '

Doyle, pretending to feign conceit, feigned more than the mere words pretended. 'They all do, my son . . . '

Cook shook his head, seeing it was impossible to get sense out of Ray Doyle on a day like this, and went out, calling: 'See you.'

Bodie, automatically, called: 'Take care.'

'Ciaou,' said Doyle.

Cook ran down the stairs.

The two partners started in on folding the scope and collapsing the tripod, boxing up the kit, clearing up. It was all wearisome routine. Casually, hefting the camera, Bodie said: 'What's she like?'

Doyle looked up. 'June? Not your sort.'

Bodie looked alarmed. 'What's that mean?'

Doyle smiled. 'Well – she's attractive – intelligent – witty – got personality – not your sort at all – '

Bodie picked up a bedroll and hurled it at Doyle. Doyle caught it, and pretended to stagger under its weight. It was one of those days, irksome routine making you fool around.

Organising the temporary release from custody and getting Jimmy Kilpin into the transit van were not the difficult items. Driving down into Kent and finding the right village and the right road were not the difficult items. Cook could still feel a bit of the old stiffness dogging him; the obbo had been useless and it had made him more than a trifle tired. Allison, in command, an older man with grown children, would drive his men if he had to. They were not the difficult items. The difficult item was putting up with Jimmy Kilpin at all . . .

The transit pulled in and when Kilpin alighted he glanced around apprehensively.

'Which way now?' demanded Allison. His men started in on unloading the van. Kilpin pointed up a narrow track leading past a small wood and over a rise. 'Come on boys, let's go,' said Allison. He spoke to Jones, who was driving. 'Alan, mind the shop. Tell 'em we've arrived.'

'Okay, skip,' said Jones, irreverently, and as the party started up the track he got on the R/T to report in.

Kilpin led them over the rise and around beyond the little wood. Distant church bells blended a golden note into the sunshine, mingling with bird songs and the hum of insects. The track wended between hedgcrows, bright with colour, and the men slogged along quite cheerfully, each one suddenly aware of the beauty of the countryside and of how seldom they had the opportunity of indulging in its peacefulness.

Among the digging equipment and a few bottles for thirsty work, Allison carried a carbine slung over his shoulder. CI5 was, after all, tangling with terrorists. The incongruity of the weapon in the idyllic countryside caught forcefully at Cook, slogging along with the shovels.

When the party reached a tall trcc, Kilpin swallowed, nodded nervously, and the men thankfully dumped their loads. Their relief was short-lived, for Allison, carbine on shoulder, got them digging tout-de-suite. They struck the first pick blows where Jimmy Kilpin indicated.

The soil came up dry at first, crumbly, shovel work. Then it hardened and the picks went in with a thwunking sound. Allison looked at Kilpin.

'You sure this is the right place?'

'Sure.'

Kilpin was still apprehensive. He glanced around the area, across the men digging, past the tall tree. The sound of the picks and shovels broke harshly into the sunshine; all the birds had flown away from this spot.

The diggers changed places, the pickaxe man handing the tool across and climbing up for a breather, the shovel man shifting another load before coming up.

Shadows from the clouds and trees drifted across. The metal of the spades grated on grit in the dig. Allison wiped his forehead with the back of his hand. Kilpin looked around . . .

He saw . . .

Shapeless in sweatshirt and jeans, unidentifiable in stocking mask, a man appeared from the shadow of the trees, his gun levelled. Sweating, shaking, Kilpin glared around. Five other figures appeared, surrounding the men in the dig, six weapons aimed. Kilpin threw up his arms in terror.

A woman's voice slashed out.

'Drop!'

Like a sack of coal Kilpin threw himself down.

The terrorists opened fire.

It was a massacre.

Allison, diving flat to the side, managed to get off a shot. He thought he hit one; but then bullets stitched into him.

All the CI5 men had been hit, all lay lax, unmoving.

Kilpin, prostrate on the ground, looked up as the woman advanced on him. He looked sickly at the S.M.G. she carried with so negligent an elegance.

She half-lifted the mask.

'Get up!'

Kilpin scrambled to his knees. He recognised Ulrike.

'You,' he stuttered. His face felt hot. 'Why?'

Ulrike said: 'I've come for you, Jimmy.'

The site of the dig looked like the aftermath of a battle. Tree called across and Ulrike went to stare down on Joe, who had taken the single burst of shots the CI5 men had got off. He was in a bad way. They'd taken his stocking mask off. His face looked like last week's newspaper lying in the gutter; blood trickled from the corner of his mouth.

'Can you walk?' Ulrike sounded matter of fact.

Joe was in considerable pain; but he was a terrorist who believed in what he was doing. 'Can try,' he said with laconic courage. 'Can't I.'

Ulrike gestured. 'Give him a hand.'

Ulrike saw two of her men helping Joe to hobble off, and went back to where Jimmy Kilpin stood, most unhappily.

'Why do you want me?' he demanded.

Ulrike seemed almost amused. Her dimples deepened beside her mouth; but Kilpin saw no humour there, none whatsoever.

'Guess!' said Ulrike, and then she prodded Jimmy Kilpin with her sub-machine gun.

As the terrorists and their prisoner walked off beyond the trees, Robbie Allison was reaching for his fallen carbine. He reached and could not make it. Blood coated in his eyes, smeared his face. He stretched for the carbine and couldn't reach it . . .

The sounds of gunfire from beyond the wood sent Alan Jones to the R/T.

'Nine-six to base, over . . . Hurry! . . . '

The voice of the operator sounded Sunday-morning lazy: 'Go ahead, nine-six.'

Jones shouted into the mike: 'We've been jumped!'

The Sunday morning languor stripped away as the operator put the CI5 info service, back-up and standby squads on alert. Alpha - George Cowley - picked up the news very early and instantly turned his car. He gave his orders in a controlled voice. Having a competent party of CI5 operatives jumped by terrorists was something he found difficult to believe; it left a nasty taste in his mouth. Perhaps Sunday morning, perhaps the tiredness after that stupid fruitless obbo, perhaps - perhaps anything. Cowley spoke into his R/T, tying up loose ends.

'Tell them to confirm helicopter. Also the unit of S.P.G. as backup. With roadblocks and dog-handlers.'

He reached the point in the road where the transit had been parked, and, following Alan Jones' directions, bumped along the track. Activity was conspicuous by its absence, only Jones was tending Robbie Allison.

Cowley got out of his car and legged the remaining distance beyond the wood. The sound of a helicopter reached down, lazily, from the blue Sunday sky. He stared about at the carnage, at the dead and wounded men. Jones stood up, his face leaden.

'One dead, two critically wounded, sir.'

'Kilpin?'

A landrover with police markings jounced up, to disgorge dog-handlers. Gradually, the machine was swinging into action. Cowley watched Jones.

'No sign of him, sir.' Jones pointed off into the trees. 'Blood tracks over there. Looks as though they have a wounded one with 'em.'

Cowley nodded and called to the dog-handlers who were now quietening their dogs and bringing them to heel.

'Over there.' Cowley pointed where Jones had pointed. 'See if you can pick up their trail.'

The droning noise of the helicopter increased. The dogs put their noses down and began to haul at their leashes.

Cowley turned to Jones and then, as the helicopter, in an abrupt rush of noise, appeared over the trees, he crossed to where Allison lay. The chopper carried large Red Crosses on her sides. Her vanes glittered and leaves and grasses swirled away.

Cowley bent to Allison. The wind from the chopper whipped their hair, caught up the dust and bits of debris.

'You'll be in hospital within minutes, Robbie.'

Allison was reliving it. 'A girl. With them . . . Girl gave orders. *Girl!*'

Cowley flicked bits of dead leaves away. 'Recognise her?' Allison shook his head, a weak gesture. 'All right, Robbie. Save your strength now.'

The ambulance men from the helicopter took over, efficiently strapped Allison into a skeleton, checked him through for broken bones first, fixed a quick-drip feed and then gently loaded him into their chopper. They moved on to the next wounded man. It was all smooth and efficient and, somehow, able to remove some of the horror.

But not for George Cowley.

Not when his men had been shot at, wounded and killed.

The men carrying Joe between them, his arms over their shoulders, both felt they weren't going anywhere with their comrade. Jimmy Kilpin, for whom Joe had been shot, was pushed along. Young Tree was generous with his pushes and shoves. He'd always liked Joe. They reached the railway bridge.

The sound of a helicopter sent them rapidly into the shelter of the trees. Carefully, Ulrike stared up. The chopper passed away, whirring, and vanished. The sound died.

Ulrike let out a breath and turned to Tree.

'Cigarette.'

Young Tree took out a cigarette and lit up. Ulrike took it out of his mouth and put it into Joe's mouth. Joe lay with his back against a tree, staring out at the weather beaten bricks of the railway bridge. The wire fencing was rusted, the concrete posts rotting. Joe felt just the same.

'Anything else?'

Joe coughed, and shook his head.

Ulrike leaned forward. This was an important moment. She was aware of that. Sacrifice, wasn't that a part of the creed, the willing giving, the sacrifice of self for the common good? Joe knew that. He was a good comrade. He understood.

She kissed Joe on the forehead. He felt like ice.

'Bless you,' she said, on a breath.

The cigarette in Joe's mouth fluttered as he spoke.

'Go.'

He couldn't manage more than the single word.

Ulrike stood up. 'Come on. Let's get out.'

Young Tree felt the bemusement turn to outrage. He stared at Joe, then at Ulrike.

'We can't leave him!'

'We have to.' Ulrike sounded fierce, like a lioness over a wounded cub. 'He's finished . . . '

They all looked at Joe, sitting there, the cigarette so silly and stupid drooping from his mouth, knowing they looked on a man already dead. The grey bricks of the railway bridge looked cheerful by comparison. Then Ulrike stiffened them up, and pushing Jimmy Kilpin along, they moved off . . .

Through the railway bridge they reached the small side road. On the air, faint at first, but growing louder, the sound of dogs reached them. There were police dogs on their trail. Young Tree, running up to their muddy old shooting brake, realised that had they tried to bring Joe with them the dogs would have been on them already.

They all piled into the brake. Tree started to shake again when she wouldn't fire; the starter moaned away to itself, gnurr-gnurr-gnurr – and then, as the sound of the dogs howled up in a break of the starter – on the next try she fired. The engine roared, and was revved up brutally. The shooting brake moved off with a heavy crunching of tyres, and then headed down the road.

At the railway bridge the excited dogs dragged their handlers on. The police officers could see the shape of a man sitting with his back to a tree. His head was up and back. They approached cautiously, for he must be one of the gang, and this gang had just shot and killed a fellow officer.

When the police were set, with guns aimed, they called out.

The man gave them no answer.

When they approached, they found out why.

Joe was dead.

Others beside Joe were dead.

Bodie and Doyle, summoned by the chief, arrived in a mood of violent anger and reluctant despair. They reached the scene of the shooting when it was almost done. George Cowley remained alone with the dead man. The others had been evacuated by helicopter, and now Cowley waited for the ambulance to take his dead man.

Bodie ran up the last few yards past the trees.

The sunshine did not seem as warm and happy as it had.

'Cook?'

Cowley looked up. He nodded. Then he said: 'Reynolds and Allison badly wounded.'

Doyle had to think of what this had been all about.

'Kilpin?'

'Judging by the spent shells I'd say five, maybe six of them.' He gestured. 'One's a girl and it looks as though another's wounded.'

As Bodie said: 'Some girl!' Doyle still kept his mind on the job. Cowley was speaking in anger now.

'I want them! And I want them fast. Maximum effort. No stone unturned. You know what I mean?'

Bodie looked at the chief of CI5. 'You'll get 'em.'

And now Ray Doyle had to let it all in past the dedication to the job. He knelt down beside Cookie, and put his fingers on his eyelids, finger and thumb, gently, closing them. 'Nice cushy number in the Fraud Squad.' All Doyle's laughter fled from his voice; he sounded harsh and vindictive. 'Until he met me!'

Cowley said at once: 'No sense reproaching yourself, Doyle.'

Doyle couldn't let it alone.

'Twenty six . . . Wife about seven months pregnant with her second kid . . . '

Cowley broke in, knowing what he was doing and saying. 'Will you tell her?' As Doyle reacted, shocked, gazing back at Cowley, the chief went on: 'Someone has to.'

For a moment the tension hung; then Doyle turned away, accepting. He tugged the gold chain from Cook's neck, held the medallion in the palm of his hand. Then he stuffed it into his pocket.

The sound of the ambulance's klaxon approaching finished that for them all. Bodie allowed he was glad of that. For a moment there he'd thought Doyle was going to give Cowley a rollocking. Doyle felt badly about this, Bodie knew, real bad. And one thing was certain, he didn't envy Doyle's task in telling June Cook.

The caravan site looked just as decrepit in the sunshine. Chickens clucked around, and if the owner didn't come along and claim 'em soon, the terrorists would have pot roast chicken for dinner in the very near future.

The handcuffs the prisoner wore remained on his wrists. The only difference was that they had a chain running through them which was locked to the front bumper of the shooting brake. Ulrike had done that. She'd done that with some satisfaction.

Young Tree stood back, watching. He was still shaken by the abandonment of Joe - and his death. For the terrorists in their hideout had to assume Joe was dead by now. Ulrike was a tough lady, young Tree saw with fresh eyes, a very tough lady indeed.

Now Ulrike glowered down on Kilpin, putting the fear of the devil into him.

'They kept questioning me . . . ' He was almost sobbing. 'On and on . . . Wouldn't let me sleep . . . All the tricks . . . I couldn't help it.

'You were trained.' Ulrike sounded contemptuous. 'Capture is always a risk.'

'They twisted everything I said.'

'If you hadn't said *anything*, they wouldn't have been able to twist it!'

Young Tree, much the same as Jimmy Kilpin, had to acknowledge to himself that Ulrike was right, dead right. She began to move away, finished with the creep chained to the bumper.

'What'll you do with me?' demanded Kilpin. Desperation and fear made his voice shake.

'Do?' Ulrike stopped, looking back, hard and merciless, dominating. 'Do? We'll finish what the court began.'

When Ray Doyle pulled his Escort into the kerb opposite Cook's house the sun was still shining brightly on this golden Sunday. To match that, the golden labrador was stretched out on the bit of front garden grass beside the pram. The pram had a sunshade rigged, ivory material, with bobbles and tassels.

Doyle just sat for a bit, hands on the wheel. He looked at the house, and the pram, and the dog, and saw the sunshine. After a time he managed to summon up courage to get out and walk up the garden path to the front door. He cut around the corner of the house, past the trellis, to the kitchen door. He tapped on the glass.

June Cook was doing some cooking. The joke was not lost

on her. Her kitchen was roaring with action, with the gas cooker jets going full blast, the oven on, and mountains of goodies growing by the minute. Of course, the enormous stomach she had at the moment, bulging out under her smock like the side of a cathedral dome, got in the way. But junior in there was going to be all right . . .

She heard the tap on the window, and turned, and saw Ray Doyle.

'Ray!'

She hurried to the door and let him in, delighted to see him. She hugged him, both of them bending into the kiss.

'What a treat. Why didn't you call?'

Before Doyle could answer, June rattled on: 'Got you all to myself this time. Cookie's out on a job.'

'I know.'

'Well . . .' She put a hand on her hip and half-turned, posing, proud of her shape. 'What do you think?'

'Blooming,' said Doyle, his lips forming the word almost as a kiss, a caress.

'Liar! I looked at myself in the bath last night – I'm way over what I was with Danny, pounds over. Can you stay for lunch?' She gestured expansively to her culinary endeavours. 'See what I'm doing? Filling the freezer. You know what Cookie's like. How can you have a name like Cook and be so useless in the kitchen?'

Doyle made no attempt to break into this barrage of words. June rattled happily on.

'Anyway, I shall leave him stocked up this time. Lots of instructions – '

Now Doyle's face reflected the turmoil within him, his realisation of the happiness bursting from this woman, her concerns, the preparations for the next child, the care over her husband – and the news Doyle brought, like a black and filthy monstrous shape rising from a pit of horror – something like that. Something, certainly, to smash happiness into pieces . . .

'What's wrong?'

'Sit down, June.'

She responded to the seriousness of his tone. She put a hand to her throat. 'What?' Doyle pulled a stool from the breakfast bar and tapped it. June said, again: 'What? What is it?'

'It's Cookie.'

'Trouble?'

'Worse than that.'

'Is he hurt?'

As Doyle made no answer, could make no answer, couldn't get his concrete lips and tongue around what he wanted to say, June realised, guessed, sensed – *knew*.

'No.' She shook her head. 'No.' This was a nightmare that would go away if she denied it strongly enough. 'No. No – I don't believe it.'

'Listen to me – ' began Doyle.

The noise of a thousand waterfalls broke into June Cook's head. She covered her ears with her hands. 'I don't want to listen! Don't tell me! Go away!' She was becoming hysterical, shaking her head from side to side, her face distraught. 'It isn't true! I don't want to know.'

Doyle moved to put a comforting arm around her shoulders, a gesture he recognised as futile but which was a human reaching of mutual sympathy. But June Cook reacted with hysterical unpredictability – or, perhaps, with a terrible predictability of grief.

'Get off!' She shouted now. 'It was you! *You* talked him into it. More money, more chances. You bastard!'

With the galvanic actions of despair motivated by unthinking vengeance June seized up a saucepan from the stove. It steamed. She swung around, holding it with both hands above the swell of her stomach, heaved the lot at Doyle. He managed to duck away, shattered. Bolognese sauce ran down the wall and curtains. The smell smoked richly into the kitchen.

'Bastard! Bastard – it's all right for you, you creep. You don't have anyone – any kids, any wife. You can go on playing cowboys all your miserable, bloody selfish life!'

As though all her energies had been chopped by this sobbed outburst, she collapsed against the breakfast bar, flopping sideways helplessly, sobbing uncontrollably.

Doyle did what he could to make her comfortable and called in Mrs Hanson, the next-door neighbour, and did not leave until he was satisfied that June was in good hands. What she had said was, of course, undeniably true. Doyle accepted that, as did Cowley and Bodie. All they could do was point to the other side of the equation.

The remand prison appeared no worse than any other, which was saying something for it, and the prison officer who showed Bodie into Kilpin's cell was clearly a smart and dedicated man. He wanted to help.

'He would've come back here?'

'Then off to court again tomorrow.'

'All right if I look through his stuff?'

The prison officer glanced at the few books, papers, letters, and said: 'Such as it is.'

Bodie turned the stuff over - uselessly. He stretched and looked at the prison officer.

'D'you know him?'

'Not really. Used to oversee his exercise, that's all.'

'Any friends?'

'Mr Bodie. You turn Queen's Evidence, grass on all your mates - doesn't exactly put you in the Charts.'

'Rephrase the question. Any enemies?'

The prison officer's mouth twisted. 'Like the whole of E Wing?'

'Somebody got a message to him. Who? How?'

'Could've happened at the Court. Grapevine operates, even here. Had a visit from his brief yesterday.'

'Yes?'

'Just routine. Brief and his client, private.'

'What's the brief's name?'

'Hockley.'

'Tim Hockley?' Bodie's face tightened.

'None other.'

'King,' said Bodie with a snap. 'Of the Bleeding Hearts.'

The prison officer knew a little of Hockley's reputation, the way he handled cases and, as often as he could, made the police look dummies. He was one of a breed.

'Whatever was said, it seemed to gee up young Jimmy.'

Bodie nodded. This was just another little item; probably of some significance, not a lot. But it would have to be slotted into the big picture, just a part to fit in with what Cowley might dig out. As for Ray Doyle; leaving the remand prison, Bodie shook his head. He didn't envy his partner the job of telling June Cook the news.

The parts of the big picture that George Cowley might find to fit in could be picked up here, in Jimmy Kilpin's home. George Cowley walked with Ross Kilpin, Jimmy's father, and Tessa, his sister, in the grounds of their Weybridge house.

Immaculately-kept tennis courts were being played on by immaculately-expert players. Cowley gave them a single hard stare and got back to the job in hand. The money here might be of a stupendous value; Ross Kilpin was just a man. He looked the part, a touch of silver at the temples, a heavy face, port-wineish, a dogmatic thrust to the jaw. His daughter, Tessa, Jimmy's sister, appeared to be a product of late-upper-class wealth. A face well-fleshed, with a pouting mouth, heavy make-up in the evening, no doubt; but now not a scrap. She could be a surprise. Cowley had experience in that direction.

Ross Kilpin was talking, his words carrying a heàvy authority no matter what he said. 'So you've heard nothing? He must have been led into it – appalling!'

'Not a word.'

Kilpin spoke with extra emphasis. 'What if I offered a reward? A substantial reward?'

Cowley made a small dismissive gesture. 'You'd get calls from every crank and halfwit in the country.'

'But would it do any good?'

'Doubt it.'

The sound of the tennis players broke in a cackle of triumph and the call of the score. The three people walking by the path totally ignored the tennis. Kilpin shook his head, dogmatically plodding on with his idea.

'I think – *if* I might say so, Mr Cowley – you underestimate the purchasing power of the pound.'

His daughter gave him a suppressed look of fury and bitterness.

'Translated literally,' she said, the bitterness spilling over into her voice so that Cowley regarded her with greater attention. 'Every man has his price.'

Cowley inclined his head to her, the sunlight catching in the sandy waves of his hair, gleaming.

'*You* believe that?'

'No. But my father does.'

Ross Kilpin glowered at Tessa. He started what must have been a familiar harangue to his children, in tone of voice and dogmatic assertion, even if the subject matter he laid down the law on for Cowley might be different.

'An issued share capital of fifteen million. Reserves of a hundred and twelve million. Seventy three thousand shareholders. Thirty eight thousand employees. Six million square feet of storage space . . . He knew the ramifications of his empire. 'I have to disagree.'

Cowley spoke in his plummiest voice, smooth, urbane, a man able to confront this blatantly exposed wealth with sources of power of his own.

'Mr Kilpin, you miss the point. Jimmy belongs to a generation in revolt against richness, vast wealth, privilege.'

Kilpin's heavy face drew up into lines that indicated he found something amusing, and was as a result laughing. Cowley eyed him.

'Why do you laugh?'

'The only dirt Jimmy ever saw was mud on the playing fields of Eton.'

'Half-baked, maybe,' Cowley agreed with the judgement made. 'But idealism nonetheless.'

The bleeper in Kilpin's pocket went off, its note a reminder of the electronic tentacles forever surrounding top people, and Kilpin excused himself and walked off towards the terrace under the arbour. There were plug in telephones up there, plus glasses and iced drinks. Tessa continued to walk along the paths between the flowers with Cowley. The tennis players sent up a background of noise completely inconsequential. She turned her face towards him, brooding, and then looked back again towards the riot of flowers in the borders.

'You're wasting your time.' She spoke jerkily, on a breath, as though driven to it.

'Am I?'

Almost in disbelief at what she was saying and the reasons for that, Tessa said: 'Three people shot - all because of Jimmy.'

Cowley considered the statement for a moment. Then, decisively, he nodded. 'If you choose to look at it that way - *yes*!'

Tessa closed her eyes, walking, feeling the sunshine on her forehead. This man Cowley seemed to her compact, competent, able to bring something to her life she had hitherto been totally unaware existed. But, she could not put a name to what it was that Cowley brought, except, perhaps, danger. And that was trite . . . She opened her eyes.

'Why would they want him?'

Cowley didn't like what he had to say; it was a hauling down of the flag, if you believed in flags anymore.

'Snatching him from under our noses - it's a coup. Be front page all over the world.' Now he was saying them, the words sounded just as bad as he'd expected. 'Another kick in the teeth for Law and Order.'

Tessa could see that, and see how her father related.

'My father - he'll never admit to anything. The infallibility of the pound . . . It's remarkable!'

'How did a lad like Jimmy get involved with terrorism?'

Tessa nodded towards her father, on the terrace with his telephones. 'Corrupted by affluence? Daddy does a lot of entertaining. One time, half his guests seemed to be servants of the law - judges, J.P.s, barristers. Hard not to conclude that the law is the prerogative of the rich.'

Cowley said, quite simply: 'Hard to think that shooting three men - in a field on a Sunday morning - does much for his case.'

He looked at Tessa, waiting for a comeback. There was no comeback from Tessa Kilpin.

Chapter Five

Back in the 'thirties they'd have called the block of flats Ritzy. All low slung cars outside, bonnets longer than seating, girls in cloche hats, short skirts, Henry Hall on the wireless, or more likely the Western Brothers, all dashing about and having fun and never mind what was going on on the Continong. The flats were still Ritzy, in their own way.

Doyle sat in the passenger seat of the White Capri looking at the flats, seeing the way the late sun threw angles of shadow. The pavements were grey and dry. Bodie walked soberly from the telephone box on the corner. He opened the door of the Capri, got in, slammed the door, said nothing.

Doyle looked at him.

Bodie said: 'Reynolds.'

'When?'

'Twenty minutes ago. On the operating table.'

Doyle thought of Cookie, and now Reynolds, Two good men gone down the grey pathway to hell and beyond. He couldn't say anything for a moment. After a bit he said: 'Allison?'

'No change.'

Bodie and Doyle sat in the white Capri, in the late sunshine of a golden Sunday afternoon, and thought about various different items of life, like guns, and blood, and death, and friends they'd never see again. If that lay at the end of the road for them, as it probably did, who were they to complain? Presently, Doyle shifted on the seat. He looked at Bodie with a speculative lift of his eyebrow.

'Don't want a dog, do you?'

Bodie was surprised. 'Dog?'

'The Cooks have one. Golden labrador.' Doyle looked at the flats in the afternoon sunshine. 'She asked me to shoot it.'

Bodie waited a moment, then: 'What would I do with a dog?'

Another heavy silence lay between them.

A new Porsche pulled in towards the flats very fast, swinging around, very spirited. It halted and Hockley got out. He went around to the passenger door, opened it, and helped a girl out. Bodie looked. She was tall, willowy, blonde. She belonged on the front page of a glossy woman's magazine; probably she had never bothered to think of that. Hockley closed the door, picked up a picnic basket from the rear, and then walked with the girl into the blue shadows under the porch.

Doyle said in his half-amused way: 'Lovely day for a picnic.'

Bodie said: 'Lovely!' He looked at his watch. 'Give him five minutes to get her dress off.'

Doyle sounded dubious. 'Long as that?'

Bodie smiled. His smile, of the wolfish kind, conveyed exactly that he was allowing five minutes to someone else, that for him five minutes would be a gross over-estimate.

Unhurriedly; but moving with purpose, the partners left the Capri and went up to Hockley's flat. Doyle leaned on the buzzer.

'Remember,' he said to Bodie. 'Lay one finger on him – '

Bodie nodded, tight-faced. 'Every lawyer Civil Liberties can lay their hands on . . . I know!'

The door opened. Hockley, in shirt sleeves and holding a frosted glass in his free hand, stared down his nose at them.

Doyle opened the batting.

'Mr Hockley?'

'Yes.'

'Sorry to trouble you, sir, on a Sunday evening – '

'I,' interrupted Hockley in an unpleasant way, 'know what day it is.'

Doyle said: 'We're officers with CI5.'

'My commiserations,' said Hockley, and his smirk was almost unnoticeable.

Bodie said: 'May we come in?'

Hockley hesitated. He was a smooth operator, knowing the score, and he was, perhaps, at this moment just a leetle undecided . . .

Doyle nudged him along. 'More private than out here in the hall.'

Eventually, Hockley stepped back. The partners followed him in, shutting the door behind them.

They took in the pad. The flat was palatial, with a deal of fine furniture, the latest in display aids, discreet lighting, low tables of glass and onyx, sheer drapes at the windows. The TV was on, the sound turned right down, and Doyle nodded to the set.

'I take it you heard the news.'

'On the car radio.'

Bodie said: 'Jimmy Kilpin's a client of yours. You were helping with his defence?'

Doyle added: 'Retained counsel, etcetera?'

Hockley remained ice cool. 'When do you tell me something I don't know?'

Doyle smiled a Doyle smile that made him look ten years younger, curly hair and all. Bodie burned a Bodie burn that made his smooth handsome features appear ready to explode.

'Had you any idea,' said Doyle in his placatory way, 'today's events would happen?'

Hockley looked incredulous, as he had every right to be.

'Is that a serious question?'

The partners continued the pressure now they'd started.

Doyle looked pointedly at Bodie. 'Neither of us is laughing.'

'Three men shot,' said Bodie, 'two dead, the other on the danger list. Not much of a joke.'

'No,' said Hockley. Suddenly, he revised his opinion of these two. They were dangerous.

'You visited Kilpin yesterday.'

'Correct.' Then Hockley looked hard at the partners, 'I see. You're linking the two items.'

'Reasonable assumption, wouldn't you say?' said Doyle.

'You were with him at three. He saw the Prison Governor at four – ' said Bodie, when Hockley, his face tight with triumphantly-controlled passion called out.

'Jackie!'

Bodie stopped talking as the tall fair-haired girl came in.

She wore a kimono, and she sauntered in, moving with a smoothness of line and economy of effort it had taken her a long time to perfect. But, for all the shining artificiality of her, she did warm up the old cockles of the heart. Bodie looked, so did Doyle. And Tim Hockley went on speaking with that vindicative bite in his voice.

'Hang around, will you, Jackie, till these gentlemen have gone. We'll have a witness, just for corroboration.' He eyed the partners. 'You were saying?'

Doyle pushed on with the interview. 'You saw Kilpin yesterday. *Why?*'

'I,' said Hockley after very little thought, 'don't have to answer that.'

'Look odd if you don't.'

With that dry note of mockery strong, Hockley almost laughed at Doyle. 'That would distress me - no end ...'

Bodie eased in with a smooth: 'Hate you to be distressed.'

Again Hockley received that fragmentary impression that these two were not the clowns they appeared, that they were dangerous. He felt he could give a little.

'Kilpin was worried about counsel - wondering if he was receiving the best advice. He showed a classical paranoia. I just went to reassure him.'

'Was it on your advice he turned Queen's Evidence?'

'No comment.'

'Could any of his revelations have embarrassed you?'

'No.'

'What'll happen to him now?'

Hockley stared up, challengingly. 'I know no more than you do.'

Doyle said: 'They went to dig up some guns.'

'Really?'

Doyle's lips pursed up. He stared sideways at Bodie, speaking hard, letting this creep, this King of the Bleeding Hearts, know he wasn't fooling them. 'Really. Sounds like he was set up, doesn't it?'

The solicitor merely gave a dismissive shrug, so Bodie prodded with: 'I wonder who'd do that to him?'

'Wouldn't have been difficult for you,' said Doyle. 'Would it? In his confidence and all that.'

Hockley put his glass down on a table. He spoke with a force he felt, a force he made no attempt to disguise.

'I think this has gone far enough.'

Bodie carried out a typical Bodie de-fusing of the heated situation. Operatives of CI5 could get away with a very great deal, and this creep deserved to be turned over, and they had a good idea they were on to something with him – but they couldn't be sure. Not absolutely *sure*.

So Bodie nodded his sleek head at the picnic basket.

'You had a good picnic anyway.' He glanced around, ostentatiously taking in the luxurious furnishings. 'You're on call to your local Law Centre?'

'As you well know.' Hockley sounded most stiff-necked.

'That pay for the Porsche,' enquired Bodie, 'does it ... some of this?'

Hockley's bristling hostility now seemed to create a hedgehog wall of spines around him. 'I imagine you can see my annual Tax Return. *If* you haven't already done so.'

Doyle wanted to find a way around that wall of spines, that bristling hostility; he was almost a hundred percent certain this brief was crooked and was mixed up in the whole unsavoury business. He tried a new tack. He wandered across to the bookshelves and read of some of the author's names.

'Marcuse ... Lao Tse ... Hegel ...'

'I do some spare-time book reviewing.' Hockley's sarcasm burned. 'Is that all right?'

Doyle picked out a book, held it up. The cover bore the name of Tim Leary. Doyle said: 'You read this?'

'Bit of it.'

'Somewhere, I believe, he says: "to shoot a genocidal robot policeman is a sacred act." Any comment?'

Hockley said: 'Depends what you mean by sacred.'

'Also depends on what you mean by genocidal and by robot.'

If you were the chief of an organisation which sent men and women out to face the possibility of death, then it was no good shirking the full responsibility of the aftermath. George Cowley, as chief of CI5, the Squad, the Big A, went to see Robbie Allison suspended among the drip feeds and swatched in bandages. The nurse gave him the usual caution. After a few words of general comfort – as ever hollow and yet meaningful in varying degrees – Cowley produced half a dozen photographs of well-known girl terrorists. Allison looked at them slowly and carefully.

When the photograph of Ulrike came up, Number five, Allison said without hestitation: 'That's her.'

Cowley tapped the glossy.

'You're sure?'

'Positive. That's one face I won't forget.'

Cowley read off the statistics. 'Judy Wynant, now known as Ulrike Herzl. Convent educated, bilingual, finished in Switzerland. According to D.S.T. report working in Germany. Possibly involved in Diplomatic Shooting in The Hague.' Cowley took his glasses off and looked at Allison in his medical cocoon. 'No doubt in your mind?'

'None at all, sir. The boy was scared. He didn't want to go with them.'

'Not surprised.'

Allison wanted to know about Brian Reynolds. Cowley shook his head. 'Never recovered consciousness.'

Allison looked bewildered, weak and helpless in the hospital bed. 'They were so young. They weren't much older than my two . . .'

After a few more words, Cowley left Allison in the hospital. There were things to be done. H.Q. tracked Mrs Wynant's current address to a hotel in Kensington. Thither Cowley drove. Ulrike's mother presented the appearance of a wealthy woman, choosing to dress in a fawn twin set with matching pearls, her hair a miracle, her complexion, in the shadow of fifty, still good. She met Cowley in the hotel lounge and took refuge behind a silver tea service.

'Neither my husband nor I has heard from Judy.'

'What about her trust fund? Money left by her uncle.'

'Not a penny of it's been touched!' Mrs Wynant, Cowley realised, did not understand the true situation.

He said: 'Mrs Wynant. Two of my men are dead. A third is seriously injured –'

'I'm sorry. Obviously I'm sorry.' She put two more lumps

of sugar into her teacup. That made six lumps by Cowley's count. 'I don't accept it had anything to do with Judy.'

Mrs Wynant tended to fidget. She fidgeted with her pearls, she kept going to fidget with her hair and then remembering its construction and cost, she fidgeted with her teacup and piled in more lumps of sugar. Cowley leaned forward. He spoke to Ulrike's mother quietly, trying to make her see that anything she might tell him that would help him, would also assist Judy Wynant. 'You see, Mrs Wynant. She is with this group. Probably in command of it.'

Mrs Wynant looked dazed, unbelieving. 'Judy back in England?' She shook her head, fidgeting. 'I don't believe you. You're – ' She sounded unreal now. 'You're trying to frighten me.'

Cowley did not sigh. But his face expressed deep concern, compassion, the drive of a man trying to force unwelcome thoughts home into unreceptive skulls. 'Why, what reason?' The waiter hovered and Mrs Wynant dealt with him. 'Mrs Wynant, your daughter is in danger. Serious danger. Best thing that could happen is for her to be arrested.'

'That's your version, Mr Cowley.'

The chief of CI5 could not keep the sharpness out of his tones. *'What's yours?'*

Mrs Wynant almost broke her string of pearls; then she simply ignored Cowley's words. He went on: 'Where'd she learn German?'

'We had German au pairs ... housekeepers ...' As Cowley nodded to himself, clearly slotting that fact into his picture of a spoiled brat neglected by her parents, Ulrike's mother flared up defiantly. 'We *had* to have au pairs! Bill's work took him abroad ...' At Cowley's hard look she went on in a furious complaint: 'My God! You people ... Social critics, marriage counsellors. Is there nothing you can't do?'

Cowley pressed the point of all this, pulling this woman into consideration of her daughter's future now.

'So she gets away – *this time.* Even get out of the country. How will it end? How *can* it end?' Cowley gestured half-irritably, 'That bedroom you're keeping aired, the wardrobe of clothes – she won't be coming home. It's not going to happen.'

'You sound so sure -'

'She's a murderess.'

Mrs Wynant looked away, catching sight of her reflection, and patting that miracle construction of hair quite unnecessarily. She was quite out of her depth in all this.

Cowley went on speaking evenly.

'She's even changed her name, you know that? Not Judy Wynant any more.'

The waiter finished hovering and presented a saucer with the bill. Mrs Wynant slapped a fiver on the saucer and waved the man away. She looked like a Pekinese disturbed from before the fire.

'I don't know much about terrorists. But I know that much! Reject your family, change your name. So easy to reject things today.' All the bitterness gathered in the shadow of fifty years clouded her words.

Cowley reacted, not altogether to his own surprise, with an attempt at kindness.

'We did it.'

She glanced up, shocked. 'Rubbish!'

'Of course we did.'

'I adored my parents.'

She crumbled a cube of sugar between her fingers. She was trembling. Cowley watched, carefully. 'Your parents were probably, what? - staunch, small town, conservative? I know mine were. You rebelled against them, them and their cliches. You flirted with Leftism, a parlour pink liberal. *I was.*' The half-bantering tone with which he brought to mind long-dead days and long-dead ways hardened as he brought the picture up to date. 'This mess is nothing like that, Mrs Wynant. This is not a phase, this is not a pose. This is anarchy - nihilism - wholesale murder!'

And, even then, after that, Cowley felt he could not believe Mrs Wynant had taken it all in. In her fawn twin-set, her pearls, sitting with the silver tea service, crumbling the cubes of sugar, fidgeting, she was like an exhibit in a museum of the day before, a museum catering for exhibits no longer viable in the world of those exhibits' children.

'I can't help you,' said Mrs Wynant. 'I'm sorry.'

Cowley stood up. He held the back of the chair. He looked down on the miracle of hair construction, seeing the scattered crystals of sugar across the table cloth.

'I don't want your help. It is your daughter who wants it!'

Ulrike was absolutely determined to make this a serious, solemn, profound occasion. She so passionately believed in the cause, and she wanted all her associates to share the fervour of her own belief. They believed in what they were doing, she knew that and they knew that; but here, in the case of this miserable Judas, lay an opportunity to grasp at a transcendental moment. Ulrike felt uplifted, shining with power. Also, the trial would convince any fainthearts of the seriousness of the mission.

The orchard smiled around the caravan site. Hens clucked. The table had been dragged out, dirty and stained as it was, and Jimmy Kilpin stood chained up to a tree. At the opposite end of the table Ulrike sat on a ricketty chair. The rest of the terrorists stood around. They were to act as the jury. The sun formed shifting patterns across the stained table, dark and light green movements, swirling among the marks. Jimmy Kilpin felt he might become hypnotised by those writhing shapes and shadows. What Ulrike was saying was past all sense to him.

'James Kilpin,' said Ulrike. 'You are charged on indictment that on or about the second week in April you – in return for certain inducements – did turn Queen's Evidence and fink on various friends and colleagues of yours. As a result of this, these former friends will all receive more severe sentences than otherwise might have been expected. How say you, James Kilpin, are you guilty or not guilty?'

All their faces turned towards Kilpin. Young Tree, acting as judge, played around with a folded wadge of newspaper, pretending it to be a judge's wig; but he quickly shrugged it off. The situation might be absurd; it was sinister and would be deadly.

'How say you, James Kilpin, are you guilty or not guilty?'

Kilpin licked his lips. He was nervous. He felt rotten, his clothes were in a mess and the rotten handcuffs were chafing his wrists sore. He licked his lips again, but spoke up courageously enough.

'You're sick - the whole bloody lot of you!'

'How say you - guilty or not guilty?'

'You're worse than the Law -' Kilpin was sweating. The reality of this farce was beginning to get to him.

Young Tree spoke up.

'Members of the Jury, because there has been a considerable amount of publicity about this case, I would like to instruct you that you must close your minds to everything except what will take place in this court. I'm sure that you will do your duty conscientiously.'

A few of the terrorists laughed; to some the words in this incongruous setting struck home shrewdly with remembered terrors. For others the farce needed to be played out to a swinging end. They stared wolfishly at Kilpin.

He burst out: 'This is mad - stark raving mad!'

Tree said sternly: 'The prisoner - in his own interest - will remain silent.' He looked towards Ulrike.

Ulrike, effortlessly falling into the part, said: 'May it please you, my lord, I appear in this case for the prosecution.'

The sunshine weakened for a moment, not exactly blotted out by cloud as having some of that golden-edged glitter frittered away by a drifting mist. A little chill gusted across the clearing in the orchard by the caravans. The farce went on, the terrorists playing their parts, Ulrike fierce and demanding, Tree acting up as the Judge. Eventually, when they felt they had done enough, Tree turned to the terrorists.

'Members of the jury, are you agreed upon your verdict?'

The terrorist acting as Foreman of the Jury nodded.

'We are.'

'How say you then - do you find the prisoner, James Kilpin, guilty or not guilty?'

'Guilty, my lord.'

Putting on a grey, grim, long-jawed face, young Tree faced Jimmy Kilpin. The terrorists now no longer regarded this trial as play-acting. They had lived it. They believed it. This was as Ulrike wished. Tree spoke in a heavy fashion.

'Prisoner at the bar, you stand convicted. Have you anything to say why the court should not give judgement according to Law?'

Kilpin remained incredulous that they should carry on like this. In this highly incongruous setting he did not fully perceive what Ulrike was making the terrorists see and feel; he was not fully one of them nor one of those chosen for Ulrike's vision.

'You're all crazy! Mad! What d'you think you're doing?'

Young Tree ignored the outburst.

'James Kilpin, you have been found guilty by a jury of your fellow countrymen. With that verdict I cordially agree. I do not propose to waste words on you. All that remains for me to do now is to pass sentence upon you.'

Ulrike stared upon Jimmy Kilpin, her gaze transparent, seeing him as he was, miserable, dirty, handcuffed, frightened, and seeing him as a cipher, a warning, a very real portent of the power she wielded. She held herself, hugging herself, waiting for young Tree to perform the final sentencing.

Tree said: 'You will suffer death in the manner authorised by the Law.'

'Amen,' breathed Ulrike, fervently.

Kilpin glared about on the terrorists. The hens scuttled about, totally disregarded. The sun shone. But, Kilpin looked about with new eyes. Now – now he was afraid! He swallowed and tried to speak, and swallowed again. The chain rattled as his handcuffed hands shook.

'Death!'

'What did you expect?' Ulrike lashed him with her contempt. She could feel the goodness in her now. 'A big wet kiss?'

'You going to murder me?'

Ulrike shook her head vehemently. 'Not murder! No! *Execute!* We reckon your testimony will add fifty years to their sentences. You've deprived them of fifty years of life. We're going to do the same to you. That's fair, isn't it?'

Identical copies of the cassette recording were sent to The Times, Reuters, and I.T.N.

Among those who listened intently to Ulrike's voice on tape were Tim Hockley. He listened intently early on the Monday morning, for he had been delivered his own cassette recording of Ulrike's voice.

'... we've suffered the violence of the system for too long. The legal system in this country is a perversion of the word "justice".' Here in Ulrike's speech, Hockley smiled. 'The law protects corporate crime, big business, the multinationals, the rich, the powerful. At the same time it persecutes the helpless and the idealistic. It victimises the poor. The law has nothing to do with justice.'

Others who listened to the fierce passionate voice were Cowley, Doyle and Bodie. They listened with none of the smiling pleasure evinced by Hockley.

'Courts are built on and sustained by lies, establishment lies, bourgeois lies, media lies, parental lies. The system cannot be reformed. It can only be broken. The system of encouraging so-called villains to rat on one another - hardly the public school ethic - a system whereby one man buys his freedom at the expense of others - what system is this? What has that to do with justice?'

The voice from the cassette-player's loudspeaker paused. A hissing hiatus, then Ulrike went on and the note of triumph was unmistakable: 'Well, we've removed your super snout, your jumped-up Judas. Removed him, like one removes a growth, a malignant growth. Organised militant struggle and organised terrorism go side by side. These are the tactics - '

At that point Cowley switched off.

'Etcetera, etcetera, etcetera.'

Bodie said: 'What about Kilpin?'

'You're a gambling man, Bodie. What do you give for his chances?'

Bodie indicated it wasn't worth answering as Doyle mentioned Ross Kilpin's offer of reward money.

Cowley nodded. 'He overlooks one thing. The terrorists are not short of money. Capitalised by the K.G.B., trained by the P.L.O., so we believe, it's the terrorists' Eton and Trinity.'

Cowley picked up a file as Doyle, going back to the potential reason behind Ulrike's recent actions, said: 'A direct attack on the legal system.'

'That's right, Doyle. Apart from routine political flak

against the S.P.G. and ourselves –' He checked the file, pulling his heavy glasses down with his habitual gesture. 'Justice Montefiore last month – seemed like a one-off, *at the time.* A jury member nobbled at the Whiteman murder trial. Famous Q.C. mysteriously refused to plead his client, mental breakdown, *we thought.* Clerk of the court committed suicide.' He replaced the sheet in the file. His voice carried that plummy ring; 'Nice pattern emerging.' He took off his glasses, flicking them shut with a bent wrist. George Cowley, chief of CI5, saw more clearly than most that nasty pattern emerging.

Bodie said: 'Kick the legal system over, you're well up the road to anarchy.'

Cowley nodded. 'Who was it said: "Charity begins at home. Justice begins next door"?'

Activity at the terrorist hide out mounted. Two of the comrades had liberated a car and now as Tree started in with his saw, the comrades began to rip off the old number plates. The fake ones were all ready. Young Tree fancied he had the right name for what he was doing. One of the branches had to be sawn off, and young Tree climbed the fruit tree and started in on sawing.

Ulrike played with a rabbit.

She stroked its back and kissed its ears. She took the rabbit over to the tree where Jimmy Kilpin remained still chained up. She spoke quite naturally.

'Used to have a rabbit, when I was at school. Your first two terms you could take a pet back, keep them in the cages under the trees. Rabbits, guinea pigs, mice. I used to call him Lenin.' Her heavy set mouth relaxed at this thought, half laughing she went on: 'Headmistress found out. Made me call him Winston. Didn't suit him.' Ulrike half-turned, still stroking the rabbit. 'Soon as he stopped being Lenin I stopped loving him.'

Kilpin just had to say: 'What happened to him?'

Ulrike looked surprised; the answer was quite obvious. She mimed a vicious rabbit punch, and made a neck-breaking click with her mouth. Kilpin's eyes opened wider.

'How old were you?'

Ulrike was vague. 'Nine - ten . . . '

Kilpin said: 'My father's put up a reward. It was on the radio. Why don't you let me go, collect the money?'

Ulrike smiled as Kilpin spoke, as though what he said was in a foreign language. She just said: 'Danger.'

'What about it?'

Ulrike smiled again. 'Better turn-on than any drug.'

Kilpin persisted. He was determined not to show his fear any more; he had to last out and find someone with sense enough to listen to a quarter of a million.

'Two hundred and fifty thousand,' he said. 'Pounds. You could buy all the bombs and guns you'd ever want.'

Ulrike glanced at him curiously, then put the rabbit down on the grass. Her index finger extended, pointed, her thumb stuck up; she aimed pistol-fashion at the rabbit.

'Pulling a gun on a man - greatest sexual turn-on of all.' She amended that quickly. 'No. *Second* greatest.' She jerked her outstretched hand and flicked her thumb down to the stiff forefinger. 'Killing is the greatest.'

'Did you hear?' Kilpin tried to get through to this frightening woman. 'Did you hear me? A quarter of a million will buy you all the bombs, all the bullets, all the guns - '

Ulrike interrupted brusquely. 'Don't know much, do you, comrade? It's food costs money, not weapons. You can get them free anywhere. Dozen armalite rifles? No sweat! You want a beef steak or a loaf of bread - that's different!'

She stalked away, hard-striding, swinging her hips, and started in yelling at the men to get the place policed-up. The cars were ready, the caravans ready, and the tree was ready as young Tree, having removed the offending branch, could throw the rope over in a clear area. The rope whirled high, swung over, snapped down. It looped the thick branch they had chosen. The loop at the end dangled. Tree supervised. A bench was pushed into position under the rope. Tree looked around as two of the terrorists hustled Kilpin up.

He tried to draw back; but their grip was giving him hell, and he could not twist away. He looked at Ulrike, and wished she would drop dead.

She said: 'You want a blindfold? Any last message?'

She lifted the polaroid camera.

Jimmy Kilpin drew himself up.

'I'll see you all in hell!'

'More,' said Ulrike, squinting through the camera viewfinder, 'than likely.'

They looped his neck with the rope and he stood on the bench and Tree kicked the bench away. Tree thought of Joe.

Ulrike took the pictures.

The discreet surveillance CI5 – with assistance – placed on the solicitor Tim Hockley paid dividends. No one likes a bent copper, and no one likes a bent brief. The Embankment could afford pleasure in a variety of ways, from merely strolling along and imagining you were the Man Who Broke the Bank in Monte Carlo, to studying the shipping, dodging the gulls, chuckling at the sparrows, admiring the girls, and admiring the architecture; yes, the Thames Embankment offers a rather nice line of enjoyable education on a sunny day. And that's not counting the oldest object around, Cleopatra's Needle.

The camera on the high roof of a building set back behind the gardens over the other side of the Embankment focussed on Tim Hockley as he opened the door of a telephone booth. He carried a large manila envelope. The door closed.

In the telephone box Hockley dialled out the local nick's number and when he had the sergeant's attention, told him the score, finishing with: ' . . . an envelope of photographs which I think you might find interesting. Anyway, I'll leave them for you.' He pushed the envelope into the phonebooks' slot and exited from the telephone booth with his usual elegant movements.

The camera followed him all the way.

He sat down on one of the seats that form part of the educational equipment of the Embankment, and watched as the police car screeched up and the uniformed men, after being very careful, at last took the envelope away with them.

Hockley stood up, and yawned, and stretched.

Easy money.

The yawn and the stretch were both faithfully recorded by the surveillance camera.

The terrorist hideout had been cleared out of most of the incriminatory evidence that forensic scientists might discover if left to poke around without hindrance. Ulrike was having none of that. Two of the terrorists went around dousing everything liberally with petrol. The other cars had already gone. The two terrorists doused inside the caravans with petrol and then climbed into the last of the cars and, with heavy revving engine, took off.

For some time - at least a quarter of an hour - the orchard remained quiet, an idyllic setting for a holiday.

From somewhere in the site came the sound of ticking.

With a bang like the Vesuvius blowing its top, one of the caravans exploded into a ball of flame. Greasy black smoke billowed. The petrol ignited. In seconds the caravan was an inferno.

As Ulrike might have said, the decadent genocidal robot cops would get no joy from *that* caravan ...

The mobile tea stall offered a good cuppa, and Bodie and Doyle drank with gratitude. They compared notes on this weird case. Doyle had gained no joy from Kilpin's sister Tessa, and now they were ready to start up any new leads the old man might have picked up in his bloodhoundy way.

'Here he is now,' announced Doyle over the rim of his cup. The Rover three and a half pelted along the road and whirled into the layby. Lorry drivers looked interestedly as Cowley climbed out; they were looking at Paula in the driving seat.

Cowley showed the partners the envelope, and as he took out the photographs, he said: 'They've executed Kilpin. They've hanged him.'

He thrust the envelope at them.

They took the photos and looked.

The tree branch was there, the overturned bench, the feel of sunshine, and Jimmy Kilpin, head all one-sided, hanging from the rope's end. He did not look pretty.

Cowley's fair hair glistened in the sunshine.

He looked mad clean through.

'That's what is known as taking the law into your own hands.'

Wilfrid Robarde allowed he was in fine fettle. He felt great. As a Q.C. reckoned by envious rivals to be wealthy, he could afford to chuckle. He walked breezily into his chambers where Martin, his clerk, was busily collating notes in preparation.

Martin, sharp, still only middle-aged, a man who knew everything he had to know and nothing more, said: 'Looked tight there for a while.'

Robarde took off his wig. He chuckled again with remembered pleasure.

'Always gives me satisfaction to put one over on Myers.'

'You,' Martin told him, 'Just like winning.'

'True.'

Robarde crossed to the window to hang up his wig. He took off his gown and hung it on the peg and then looked out of the window. The side street, always quiet by Chambers, was as usual heavily overparked. A woman driving a nice new Vauxhall was trying to park. The space was cramped, between a shiny Jaguar and a somewhat nondescript Cortina. She was tentatively backing onto the Cortina.

Robarde in his good mood was quite kind - for him.

Contemptuously, he said: 'Women drivers!'

Martin got up and went across to join the Q.C.

Together, they stared out through the window onto the woman struggling to put her Vauxhall into a parking space that might have taken a Metro - with skill.

Robarde said: 'Five pounds she doesn't do it.'

Martin looked. He knew his man. 'Make it "p", I might. No. No, on second thoughts, I don't think so.'

The woman had the wrong lock on now and her wing passed perilously close to the Jag. She must have done something else interesting, for the Vauxhall convulsed and lurched back.

Robarde said: 'Not in a thousand years!'

The sunshine lay angled across the street, picking out the gilding on the spearpoints of the railings opposite. It glittered in the ranked rows of windows. The side street was narrow, and most of the windows let some light into the chambers of barristers and lawyers and clerks.

Robarde and Martin were very possibly - even probably - not the only people watching the antics of a wretched woman trying to park her new Vauxhall in a space she had no right to expect to get into at all.

She backed and filled, and backed again.

In a movement of clear desperation, the Vauxhall lurched back. Its boot touched the boot of the beat-up old Cortina.

There was - clear and true, like distant church bells -a ringing crashing sound of metal against metal.

That clashing cymbal-like note had time to echo just once across the window-lined sidestreet.

Then the old Cortina blew up.

An enormous fountain of black smoke rose after the spiteful spit of orange flames.

Robarde and Martin were hurled backwards, blasted with the shards of their window, bashed headlong into the far wall.

Flames and smoke filled the street amid the sounds of hundreds of windows being blown in.

The burglar alarms started to go off, wailing their warnings, adding to the inferno.

Five pounds or five p - that didn't matter to Robarde or Martin, or to other people, either . . .

Chapter Six

The sidestreet presented the picture of a bomb-outrage aftermath. To the people handling the details, the business was becoming horribly familiar, and this was a familiarity they could do without. Screens covered the more grisly exhibits. Police cars with flashing blue lights choked one end of the street. Red lights going on and off in a maddening cycle, ambulances waited at the other end. Stretchers were being carried through the debris towards the waiting meatwagons.

A garage cranelorry was easing away with one of the wrecked cars, a blackened and twisted lump.

Cowley spoke to Robarde's clerk, Martin.

Martin wore a bandage around his head, sticking plasters across his face, and his shirt front was growing black and stiff with dried blood. He looked composed; but every now and then he twitched. He was building up a nasty tic in his left eyelid.

'We just stood there, watching,' said Martin. He forgot and shook his head, and winced. 'We even had a silly bet on the woman getting in, although I wouldn't take – '

'What happened?'

'She clouted the other car – '

'Which way was it facing?'

Martin was still a little fuddled. He put a hand to the bandage. He could still see the orange blossom of the explosion, the grotesque black thing at the heart of the fire. 'Which way?'

'Towards you,' said Cowley, very patiently. 'Or away?'

'Away – I think.' Martin closed his eyes. They still stung. 'Yes, it was away.'

'So they'd be boot-to-boot?'

'Yes. Is that important?'

Cowley nodded with assurance. 'Could be. Did you see the other car being parked?'

'No. I'd only been in a few moments. Five minutes before - we were both in court. And now - '

'Thank you for your help.' Cowley spoke firmly, his voice not hard but final. Martin looked dazed and then, released, trailed off to the waiting ambulance.

Going back to the Rover Cowley leaned down and was about to speak to Paula, when his R/T called.

'Alpha here. Go ahead.'

'Alpha. They've found Jimmy Kilpin's body.'

Cowley's brows drew down. He got the co-ordinates, and settled in the back of the Rover, said to Paula: 'Drive fast; but drive with due care and attention. They've blown a hole in the legal profession; now let's go and see the way they take the Law into their own hands.'

The co-ordinates led Cowley to the orchard hideout. One caravan was a mere black skeleton. The other remained. A few hens were beginning to pluck up courage after the bang and the fire to return and start grubbing around again.

Jimmy Kilpin's body had been cut down after forensics were through and he was laid gently on a stretcher and carried off to the ambulance. Cowley got out of the Rover and walked across to join Bodie and Doyle. They looked distinctly upset.

'Yes, I know,' said Cowley. 'Another snook cocked at the legal system.'

'Looks,' said Bodie, 'from the tyre tracks, as though there were three cars. Three.'

Doyle said: 'Two more mobile bomb carriers.'

Cowley nodded, looking about. The feeling of being upset chilled him. One car bomb had done a great deal of damage; two more, on the loose - 'Must assume so.'

'Legal targets,' said Doyle.

'The Bailey ... Temple ... Inns of Court ... ' Cowley shook his head.

Bodie could offer no comfort. His lips wrinkled as he said: 'Every court house in the country, virtually.'

Cowley thought about that. 'Let's say within a fifty mile radius.'

He had work to do, people to organise. This campaign of terror was moving into top gear. He started for his Rover and Bodie called. 'The incendiary device didn't go off in the second trailer.'

'Grateful for small mercies. Take a look at it, you two. See if it tells you anything.'

He climbed into his car and was immediately busy on the R/T.

The partners exchanged looks, Bodie sniffed, and they set off across the clearing for the undamaged caravan. Forensic had made sure the device was safe. A flat charred smell hung in the air. They walked past the blackened wreck, the stink gagging into their nostrils. The orchard closed in here, by the caravans. A few wooden crates and apple boxes lay about.

In the bushes to the side of the caravan where an overturned table made a square splodge of shadow, long brambles of a rich winey-red and powerful green spoke eloquently of a good blackberry season to come. Doyle froze.

'Shsh.'

Bodie stopped stock still. 'What is it?' he whispered.

'Keep still.'

For a moment the two CI5 men remained rigid, waiting, then Doyle dived headlong into the underbrush.

He avoided the worst of the prickles and bounced up, smiling hugely, cradling the rabbit. The rabbit's ears flopped.

Bodie grunted sourly, letting the tension go. His hand moved away from his gun butt.

'Supposed to come out of hats, not bushes.'

Doyle stroked the rabbit. 'Big fine chap.'

Bodie was crude.

'Look even better in a white sauce with a few mushrooms around him.'

He went up into the unburned caravan. Doyle looked after his partner, reflected that everyone in the world couldn't be born with an artistic soul, and put the rabbit down. He watched as the rabbit bounded off. Then he followed Bodie into the caravan.

Cowley gave the caravan a look, and then told Paula to drive. He settled down to sorting through the details so far known in this case, and realised that unless they were very quick, very lucky, or the opposition was foolish, the police forces were in for a very rough time. There were probably two motor cars stuffed with explosives ready to go off somewhere in London. They'd be placed so as to do the maximum amount of damage, and not just to property and people who happened to be passing by, but to the dignity and authority of the legal profession. There was a bent lawyer in the case, too . . .

Cowley fancied Bodie and Doyle ought to have another crack at that young gentleman . . .

Paula drove him to the mortuary chapel where they had begun tidying Jimmy Kilpin up, sufficiently, at least, for his father to make the official identification.

Ross Kilpin had had to deal with death before. That this was his son Jimmy was a cruel blow he'd have to come to terms with. He intended to use his money to bludgeon answers. He'd rest easier if he got the bastards who'd done this by the short and curlies. He was a man who got things done, and he made that plain as he walked away from the sheet-covered body of his son.

'I'll double the reward for information leading to an arrest.' He spoke with a jaw-chewing arrogance allied to a defiance, a spitting in the face of fate. 'Half a million! No one's that loyal!' He glared at Cowley. 'Right?'

'Mr Kilpin. Money can't solve all life's problems.'

'Solves more than you give it credit for.'

Ross Kilpin spoke with feeling. He *knew*. Lack of money stunted everything.

Cowley shook his head. 'Don't you see? It created your problem?'

'What!'

Cowley sighed, walking away from this man's dead son, sheeted, wrapped, ready for whatever lay in store. He said: 'If you'd been averagely well-off, then this would never have happened. Jimmy would have had nothing to rebel against. He would have had nothing to feel guilty about – '

Kilpin broke in to explode this nonsense.

'Cowley – my father never once had five pounds in the bank. *He* felt guilty. That was real guilt!'

They stared at each other, unable to agree. Cowley could feel the natural sympathy anyone must feel for a man who has just lost a son. But money was at the cause of this, no doubt of it. Perhaps having too much money and not having enough were both evils, both breeding reactions of guilt and anger. For whatever reasons, associates of Jimmy Kilpin were trying to blow the legal profession to pieces. Whatever reservations there might or might not be about that profession George Cowley knew that he had to do what he could to save lives and protect the innocent.

Once anarchy opened out into a flowering of bombs, the way was clear for complete chaos. So the pundits said. Maybe they were as wrong about that as this argument was wrong-headed about money. Cowley took his leave, still polite in his urbane way, the sun soft on his sandy hair. He wanted to find out how his prize pair of ruffians, his two top agents, had got on.

Bodie and Doyle went to see Tim Hockley again.

The flat looked spacious and airy, filled with fine furniture, oozing style and comfort. Onto one of the onyx and glass tables Bodie threw down his hand of photos, like playing a hand of cards.

The glossies slid and then held by static. They were all good shots. They showed the Embankment splendidly. They showed the phone box, and Hockley going in with the envelope and coming out without it. Bodie flicked the last one out.

'Takes a good picture, doesn't he, Doyle?'

'Yes.'

'Photogenic.' Bodie's neck squeezed in his collar as he turned to give Hockley a hard stare.

'All right,' said the solicitor. 'I've seen enough.' The sneer lay in his voice. 'Should I be impressed?'

'Depends,' said Doyle.

'On what?'

'How smart you are.'

Bodie said: 'You had to phone. What was wrong with your office phone?'

Hockley didn't waste time on that one. 'I happened to be out.'

Bodie laughed. He said in mocking mimicry: 'Happened to be out.' Bodie had the feeling they were closing in on this bent brief. 'Play him the tape, Doyle.'

Doyle put the mini tape-player on the table and switched on. Hockley's voice sounded loud and clear, lifelike.

'I want to talk to someone,' came the recorded voice of Hockley from the little player, 'about the Kilpin kidnapping.'

A heavy voice answered: 'Who?'

No one needed to be told the voice belonged to the policeman on the other end of the line from the Embankment phone.

The recorded voice repeated briskly: 'Kilpin. Jimmy Kilpin.'

'Hold on, sir.'

'Make it quick.'

Now a new voice sounded on the tape, that of the policeman who had taken the call. He started off by saying: 'Hello?'

The voice of Hockley on the tape cut in, speaking rapidly and precisely, not misplacing a single word.

'I'll say this once and that's all. I'm in the phone box on the Embankment corner of the steamer ferries. I have an envelope of photographs which I think you might find interesting.'

The voice finished.

Doyle reached down and switched off.

Bodie stared hard at the brief, and feeling again that sense that the hunt was closing in. Leave no stone unturned, Cowley had said. Well, in this creep they'd turned over a right specimen lurking under his stone.

'Your turn, Mr Hockley,' Bodie said, pointedly, waiting for the inevitable explanation.

Hockley sneered. 'That supposed to be me?'

'Yeh.'

'Could've been anyone from Donald Duck to Mao Tse Tung.'

'Sounded just like you to me.' He looked enquiringly at his partner.

'To a T,' confirmed Doyle.

'It would!'

Doyle told him: 'By the time they've had that in the lab and filtered out the traffic, put in a bit more base, less treble, pinch of salt ... It'll sound perfect.'

The solicitor understood what was being said. He glowered on the two CI5 men.

'In other words, a routine "Made in Britain", good old-fashioned fit-up?'

'Right!' Bodie spoke brightly, as though commending a forward child on its grasp of the multiplication table. He explained: 'Couple of Yank fragmentation grenades in your drinks cupboard – '

Doyle said, fiercely: 'You don't think Jimmy Kilpin was stitched up?' He looked disgusted. 'Poor little rich kid, all mixed up over Daddy's millions. And he finishes looking up a rope.'

There ensued a silence made all the more ominous for Hockley by reason of his own silence. At last Bodie shuffled the photos on the fancy table and spoke in a bluff, confidential, advisory voice.

'Know what I'd do, Tim? I'd be on my bike and pedalling.'

Doyle took the other stance. 'Where's your loot stashed? Switzerland? Jersey? Bahamas?'

Bodie pursed up those mobile lips and nodded his head with great judicial feeling. 'Off and running.'

Hockley peered at the partners suspiciously. He was still carrying on a rear-guard action; but even he suspected by now his defence was busted wide open.

'Why you bothering?' He looked and spoke warily.

Bodie made an expansive gesture.

'To save ourselves trouble.'

Doyle nodded, speaking his lines in that open, free, all-pals-together way he had. 'Yeah, lots of sweat and aggro.'

'Papers ... Reports ... ' amplified Bodie, piling it on. 'Back and forth to the D.P.P.'s office – '

'Easier,' nudged Doyle. 'Easier all round if you scoot.'

Hockley looked at Bodie, smooth and handsome and wrinkling up his lips, and at Doyle, cheerful and topped by an unruly mass of curls, and he felt the beginnings of the shakes.

A drop of sweat started out on his forehead.

'How do I know I can trust you?'

'You don't.'

Bodie started to shuffle the photos together.

'Before we turn a blind eye, Tim. One last question.'

Doyle said, and with a snap: 'Ulrike and her merry men. *Where?*'

'You don't think I'd know, do you?'

'Yes!'

'I've no idea.'

Displaying grave disappointment, letting Hockley see that as an act, as an awareness that the act covered just what Bodie was intending, he put on mock disappointment to say: 'Ah!'

A touch of desperation infused the brief's voice.

'They wouldn't tell me.'

In Bodie's neat way, Bodie said: 'Least he doesn't deny knowing them.'

Doyle's voice grew a little thick around the 's's, a truculence broadening his tones: 'Mission's over, is it? Mission accomplished?'

'I would've thought,' said Hockley. If there might have been a trace of smugness, he was wise enough to kill it stone dead.

'So,' said Doyle. 'What next? Up and away?'

'Probably.'

'How?'

'*I don't know*!'

Doyle said: 'Think!'

'No use . . .'

Bodie said: 'Try.'

As Hockley screwed up his face, drawing down his eyebrows in an effort to think, Doyle and Bodie waited. They had learned only confirmatory facts; there were two motor cars on the loose, stuffed with explosives. How they were to be found was the big black question mark hanging over them.

'Come on,' said Doyle, at last. 'Dublin . . . Belfast . . . Sealink out of Harwich?'

Hockley spoke haltingly. 'An airline bucket shop in

Gerrard Street. Transasiatic. The chances are they'd buy their tickets there.'

Bodie beamed.

'Good lad!'

As the partners packed up to leave, Bodie gave the bent brief a friendly squeeze of the shoulder. Bodie's fingers were strong, the squeeze hard. Hockley knew they were saying goodbye.

The vertical architecture of the Royal Courts of Justice threw splendid shadows in the sunshine. Come to that, the rest of the Courts' architecture threw splendid shadows. A police car parked opposite contained two officers who scrutinised a car parked further along. They had a good view. Alec Higgins lifted the R/T and spoke in his heavy voice in which the traces of Derbyshire were not entirely eradicated.

'I want a lost or stolen check run on vehicle Gold Uniform Lima seven four eight Lima. It's a Ford Corsair.'

The other officer in the car wore plainclothes. He was Laurence Stone, and he fancied he had a good chance of making detective sergeant real soon now, given the right opportunities.

'You mean it is now, Alec,' he said.

'The registration - seventy-two, or seventy-three -'

'Yes,' said Laurence Stone, chuckling at the impudence of it. 'And a seventy-seven car!'

That had alerted the two officers, the clumsy rigging of fake number plates, quite anachronistic in relation to the car. The operator spoke over their R/T.

'Car reported lost or stolen at Zulu Delta last Tuesday. It wasn't a Ford then. It was a Vauxhall.'

The plainclothes man nodded. This was no time for fooling around.

Stone said: 'Right, Alec. Call the Bomb Squad.'

Poke an ants' nest with a stick and the resulting effect is not too much unlike a busy airport. Frenetic activity apparently going nowhere belies the throughput of both examples of different cultures. One often wondered if ants ever adjusted to waiting. Possible; waiting is the name of the game in travel.

You wait here and you wait there and even when you're aboard your plane you wait for the flight to be over.

Cowley met Bodie and Doyle at the airport.

They all had the feeling that the screws were tightening in to the last turn. Cowley's report of the second bomb being found drew frowns of concern.

'Bottom of Fleet Street,' Cowley told them. 'In a car with fake registration. Lucky a couple of coppers kept their eyes open.'

'Royal Courts of Justice,' said Doyle.

'Aye. That's it.'

Bodie pinched his lip. 'Two down. One to go.'

Said like that it sounded even more uncomfortable.

They went with the old man into the lounge and scaled the heights of a balcony to look down nervelessly on the scene. It looked ugly down there. At any moment, you felt, a scrimmage would break out, and no oval ball to come spinning out of the scrum. Doyle went off on Cowley's instructions armed with the information they had and seeking the information they needed.

Cowley pointed out Ulrike for Bodie's benefit.

'That's her.'

She sat with another of the terrorists. They sat a little hunched up, a bit like refugees waiting for the last train for the frontier. They looked grey and pinched and yet in the swirling movements of the throngs of travellers about them they were not conspicuous. Their camouflage blended.

Doyle finished his investigations and rejoined the others at their high vantage point on the balcony. He took a good look down and around as he reported in.

'They've checked in on the evening flight to Amsterdam.'

Bodie cocked an eye at the chief.

'How do you want to play it?'

Cowley did not hesitate.

'Every minute's vital. So let's pick her up right now and start questioning her.'

Still looking over the balcony, Doyle said: 'I wonder where her mates are in that lot?'

The noise lifted up to the balcony, an incessant surf-roar hushing and booming, vaulting the high space. People sat about or moved from point to point. The kaleidoscope of colours dazzled.

'They won't be armed,' Bodie pointed out. 'They'd never get past the X-rays.'

'Let's pull her out – that'll get some reaction from the others. If they're there.'

'Leave that to me,' said Cowley.

'Come on, let's go.' Doyle eased up and nodded to Bodie. 'Low profile.'

'I think,' said Bodie as he ambled off after his partner, 'I've heard that before, somewhere.'

The CI5 agents had experience in organising a quick operation like this, and they checked with security and secured the use of a room. Doyle borrowed an official-looking form – it not only looked official, it was official; but it had nothing to do with what was going down here – and they walked through the throngs, very gently, towards the bench where Ulrike and her companion sat waiting.

Doyle put on his devoted public-servant face, very worried.

He stopped by Ulrike and pointed to the Amsterdam sticker on her hand luggage.

'You on the 17.50 to Amsterdam, miss?'

Ulrike looked up, just a little startled, but seeing only a further representative of this tiresome travelling system.

'Right.'

'You have your boarding pass?'

'Yes.'

Doyle began to work up the tension here, as though awaiting the outcome of a giant raffle. He hovered protectively over the girl as he said: 'What's the number?'

Ulrike pulled out her passport. The boarding card was stuck to the passport. She read, looked up, and said: 'Five nine eight.'

Doyle accepted the passport and card. He looked at the card with an expression that said, he was hoping against hope. Ulrike frowned. Doyle shook his head, as though helpless against the blows of fate. He looked at Ulrike, about to let her into the secrets of life and death.

'What sort of case've you got?'

Ulrike made it short. 'Brown and plain.'

Doyle looked crushed. He did not raise his hands to heaven and drop them in a giant gesture of despair and resignation, he did not roll his eyeballs upwards in reciprocal agony; but he might just as well have done. His voice deepened, like the doctor telling the best friend his best friend's wife has just died in childbirth.

'Sorry to tell you . . . It's burst open. Fell off the tender. Could you come down and tidy it up? Make your insurance claim.'

Ulrike sounded peevish - well, she had every right to be. 'Now?'

'Sooner the better. Don't want to delay the flight, do we?'

She thought about this. It was one hell of a nuisance; but it was better to get it all tidied up and neat, no loose ends. She stood up and Doyle, visibly relaxing, started to lead her off. Bodie said in his most polite way to the other terrorist: 'You want to help?'

The terrorist, concerned, nodded and got up to follow the others. They went off through the people in a bunch.

Against the next set of seats young Tree stood up to see what was going on. He tip-toed to spot Ulrike going off with a couple of flunkeys. His first instinctive stab of fear abated and he turned ninety degrees the other way to see the other pair of terrorists, and check their reactions. They both reacted to his concern, shook their heads, and then sat down. Tree smiled and sat down.

Watching all this byplay, George Cowley could afford a smile of his own. But, whilst the last car packed with explosives remained unlocated, this was no time for grinning like a jackanapes. He signalled his CI5 men. They had the terrorists taped, now. Now they'd wind 'em up in that tape.

In the small room Doyle had borrowed from security stood a table with a telephone. There were no papers on the desk, no files, nothing apart from the telephone.

Doyle ushered Ulrike into the room, and Bodie followed with her companion.

Ulrike saw the room, saw the bare desk, and turned on Doyle.

'What is this?'

In a tone of gravity appropriate to the occasion and what he was saying, Doyle said: 'Ulrike Herzl – Judy Wynant – you're nicked. And your friend.'

The tableau held for two heartbeats. Then Ulrike's companion moved, tried to barge past Bodie. That was a mistake. Ulrike yelled a warning, Doyle stepped out of the way, the chop of Bodie's hand was highly economical, and the companion rubbed noses with the floor. When they had that all sorted out, the partners could get down to talking to this tigress and attempt to find out what they had to know.

But Ulrike attacked first. 'Why don't you charge me?'

'We will,' Doyle told her. 'Don't rush us.'

Bodie, having seen to the companion's comfort, came back to say, putting admiration into his voice: 'Ulrike Herzl. Not every day we meet a real live star.'

Doyle nodded agreement. 'Should really be in the V.I.P. lounge.'

They paused for a moment. Ulrike remained indifferent to their comments and sarcasm. They were not going to get through her armour along those lines . . .

Bodie laid it on the line, brought it out in the open, ran it up the flagpole, gave it to her straight.

'We want to know where you left those three cars.'

Now Ulrike turned her head in a heavy, enigmatic way.

'Time will tell.'

'Oh, cryptic,' said Doyle, radiating disgust. 'Very cryptic.'

'We'd rather know *now*,' Bodie pointed out.

'We know,' added Doyle, 'they have bombs in them.'

'*How* do you know?'

'Lots of innocent people, Judy, will be killed or maimed. Young kids'll lose eyes, or limbs . . .' Doyle wasn't playing games now. 'You really want that?'

Ulrike lifted her chin. The marks at the side of her mouth never looked like dimples. A hardness glowed in a patina of suppressed violence from her. She was defiant, proud, recalcitrant – proud . . .

'*Yes*!'

The partners just looked at her. They didn't say anything for a space; but their thoughts were crystal clear.

Presently Doyle put it to her: 'Won't help you.'

'Not us; but it'll help the others.' Ulrike blazed her defiance now. 'Today - England. Tomorrow - Germany, France, Holland. In a year's time there won't be a courtroom in Europe working properly!'

They left her in the room to stew for a bit after that. Fred Tolliver came in to keep an eye on her. He was one CI5 man who wouldn't be distracted, and Polly Edwards was a CI5 lady working on the same kind of dangerous ops as the men and brought in here because she was a woman. More than one operative expressed the question, openly, if Ulrike herself was a woman or not.

They found George Cowley in the car park with a map of London spread out over the bonnet of his Rover.

Two markers marked the sites where the bomb-cars had been found; one by being accidentally hit, the other by sharp observation by patrolling policemen.

Cowley tapped a pencil against the map, letting the sharpened point wander over the various possible targets. There was a third car. It was stuffed with explosives. It was parked where it would do damage to officers of the Courts or people involved with the law.

It had to be found.

Before it blew up.

That was the job George Cowley and CI5 had to do. Once the Bomb Squad had the car, that would be it.

Doyle walked across and Cowley looked up over his spectacles.

'How's it going?'

'It's not.'

'Tough?'

Cowley took off his specs, flicked them shut and stowed them, then started rolling up the map.

'The Fleet Street bomb was set for five o'clock. Assuming this last one's the same, then we've got just another hour and a half.'

Doyle leaned against the car, looking back at the airport

buildings. His hair showed a mass of tight curls and his face looked bruised with tiredness. 'She's full of hate and very well trained.'

Cowley took the plastic bag containing Ulrike's possessions from the seat of his car and emptied it over the bonnet. He and Doyle looked moodily at the scattered items. Some loose change, paper money, the passport and card placed back by Doyle, aeroplane tickets, a wrist watch.

'Not so much as a lipstick or a comb.' Cowley poked at the wrist watch.

'No vanity,' said Doyle. 'It's all part of the non-personality cult.' He picked up the watch from under Cowley's poking finger.

Cowley spoke fretfully: 'Fifty – a hundred – lives, maybe more, at stake. And nothing we can do.'

Doyle dangled Ulrike's wrist watch by the strap.

'Isn't a clock in that office, is there?'

'No.' Cowley looked at Doyle. 'What are you thinking?'

'What,' said Ray Doyle, worrying it through even as he spoke. 'What if we give her the watch back, along with the other gear. But we put the time forward. Say an hour or so. So, when it's four –'

'She thinks it's five.'

'Right.' Doyle saw it now. 'After five, as she thinks, when the bomb should have gone off – she might – emphasise the word might – might relax.'

Cowley had it all, now. 'We can do better than that. I'll come in and tell her it *has* gone off.'

Doyle had worry enough; and he had to say: 'Think we might trap her that way?'

All Cowley said was: 'Better change your watch, too.'

Doyle nodded and turned the hands to match on both watches.

Cowley, thinking, said: 'An hour's too long.'

'You think?'

'Make it forty minutes.'

Doyle twisted the knob on his watch and a speaker of the P.A. system blasted from so near that they both jumped. Doyle pointed to the speaker which was bellowing a routine announcement – including the time.

'We'll have to fix that!'

Cowley smiled confidently.

'No problem. I'll contact the airport police. Tell Bodie what we're doing.'

'Check.'

Doyle finished up with the watches, put Ulrike's stuff back in the plastic bag, and went off to the room where she was being held. She looked up as Doyle walked in.

He looked at her. 'Nice rest?'

She merely yawned.

Doyle glanced at Tolliver standing impassively by the door. 'Okay, Fred. Get yourself some tea.'

Tolliver nodded and went off to find Polly Edwards.

Ulrike reacted to this byplay.

'I see you don't bring me any.'

'Seemed a bit mundane for you. Cup of hot hemlock –'

She cut him off sharply.

'I'd like to make a phone call.'

'Shouldn't be a problem.'

'When?'

'Later.' Doyle shut his mouth and waited, looking very bright-eyed at the girl. Then he laughed. 'I thought for a moment you'd say it was your legal right.'

She ignored this jibe at her beliefs; the test of action, clearly, she considered to be beneath her. Doyle was perfectly prepared to go along with her tough act. As if suddenly remembering after the banter he produced the plastic bag with her few possessions and placed it carefully on the table between them.

'You can keep these for the moment.'

Ulrike opened the bag and sorted through the contents. She stirred the loose change with one forefinger and then picked up the wrist watch. She glanced up.

'Should I count the money?'

'Why not?'

She had looked at the watch before she looked up at him, and Doyle guessed she was consumed by the frustration of not knowing how the time was passing and how near she was to the success of her explosive plans. Now, with the sharp remark about the money, she suddenly shot out her hand

and gripped Doyle's wrist. He just let her twist his arm so she could read his watch, then he wrenched his hand away. She bit her lip.

Doyle felt he ought to make some comment on her action, otherwise she might think it odd he did not. At last he thought to say: 'Time flies – when you're having fun.' He made it as dry as he could. If this little scheme did not work Cowley and the people of CI5 would be left with egg on their faces – and somebody would be left with a ton of bombs going off in the street right outside their windows.

Bodie pushed the door open and barged in. He was carrying a plastic cup of tea with a protective cradling action. He knew Ray Doyle.

Doyle said, brightly: 'For me?'

'Me,' said Bodie, firmly. 'One of 'em's called Tree. He's starting to talk.'

Ulrike broke in. She looked passionate, hot-eyed, defiant. 'Liar!'

Bodie, at once, with great humility, said: 'He's *not* called Tree and he's *not* starting to talk.'

The fire continued in Ulrike. She stared with open contempt on Bodie. She looked, in her heavy way, rather splendid. 'Think I'd fall for an old trick like that?'

Bodie was amused by her. 'You're right. Wasn't worthy of me.'

Doyle thought something about Bodie's attitude promised a grain of truth in what he'd said about this terrorist called Tree. 'What's he say?'

'He was the contact with Tim Hockley, the tame brief.'

Doyle nodded and glanced shrewdly at Ulrike. 'Interesting.'

Ulrike's face continued to express her contempt, her disdain, her hatred of these robotic degenerate lackeys of a pernicious system.

Bodie added fuel to the fire. 'And only *one* of the caravans blew up. You know that?'

Ulrike shook her head. 'I don't believe you.'

'True. A field day for Forensics.'

From overhead the Public Address system blasted off with the announcement of a sixteen fifty flight and Ulrike glanced swiftly up at the speaker, and then at her watch. Doyle and Bodie noted these actions without displaying any interest to the girl. Her face tightened appreciably, and she put up a hand to push back a stray wisp of hair.

She stared challengingly at the partners.

'Why don't you charge me?'

Doyle shook his head. He looked admiringly at Ulrike and then with surprise said to Bodie: 'I never knew anyone in such a hurry to get charged.'

Bodie just smiled a Bodie smile, smooth and elegant, very much like a wolf - or a shark - about to bite.

Doyle indicated he wanted to talk to Ulrike, and Bodie, taking the hint, went off to see Cowley. Doyle began to get Ulrike to open up, to let her talk, to let her get it off her chest. She was pumped full of idealistic notions, ideas based on truth and commonsense that in the present way of the world were unworkable. He wanted to get her to ask herself the question, how did blowing up policemen and lawyers and judges materially help ordinary people to a better way of life. She rambled on, fiery and passionate one moment, hard and vindictive the next.

Up on the balcony Cowley paced impatiently one way of the railed area, glanced at his watch, paced the other way.

Then he looked at his watch again.

The hands tick-tocked relentlessly along, and passed five o'clock. Bodie walked up to join the chief. For a moment they both stared at the busy scene, people hurrying to garishly coloured lockers and departure desks, and trolleys and flags and noise and bustle. It was just another day. And a car loaded with explosives tick-tocked away to itself just as Cowley's watch tick-tocked. His five o'clock had passed; the real five o'clock lay too frighteningly near in the future to risk any mischances.

'How long,' said Bodie, not looking at Cowley. 'How long you going to leave it?'

Cowley looked at his watch again.

'Another five minutes.'

That would lend credence to the news having been radioed in to the chief of CI5 at the airport. They daren't rush this one . . .

Bodie, fretful, wrinkling his lips, said: 'Do you think she'll fall for it?'

Cowley put both hands on the rail and gripped.

'If she doesn't there'll be . . .' He stopped himself. Then, in a hard voice, he said: 'Let's not even think about it.'

The conversation between Doyle and Ulrike went around in circles and reached no conclusions. Save, perhaps, that the old saw the road to hell is paved with good intentions was not far wide of the mark.

With that amused lilt in his voice, and yet with a tired feeling that he was wasting his time, Doyle said: 'So you're going to abolish poverty –'

She broke in impatiently.

'Is that such a bad thing?'

'Not at all. It has been tried before, believe it or not.'

As he spoke Doyle took from his pocket the gold chain and medallion he had removed from Cook's neck. Doyle's face expressed a mild surprise; of course he remembered putting Cook's medallion in his pocket; but it had lain there forgotten in the heat of action until now. The moment seemed to him not only appropriate but monumentally so, a fierce and biting commentary on the ideas this girl had assimilated and sought to promulgate in so savage a way.

She was going on, again, about her plans.

'We won't stop there.'

'Of course not,' nodded Doyle and the sudden new sarcasm in his tones passed her by.

'After that, we destroy repetitive, mindless, demeaning work.'

'Great!' His sarcasm now brought her head up. He looked at her, not liking what he saw. 'That, by definition, will create more poverty, no?'

She half-turned her back on him. Her face drew down. 'Waste of time arguing with people like you.'

The tannoy blared again, this time giving the flight departure time as seventeen ten. Ulrike looked at her watch. Watch and public address system tallied as to time. Watching her closely, Doyle saw the way she unconsciously relaxed. The way she sat with less rigidity in her backbone, the way she did not lick her lips so often, the way she touched her hair. She must be hugging herself with glee, surmised Doyle.

She could afford to be gracious and unbend.

She indicated the chain, glinting its golden links between Doyle's fingers.

'What's that?'

'Chain. Used to belong to someone I knew.'

Now Ulrike became condescending.

'Girl?'

Doyle refused to rise to the challenge. He shook his head and slipped Cookie's gold medallion and chain back into his pocket. He had absolutely no intention of explaining the significance of the golden chain to this girl. None whatsoever.

Pushing things along, wondering when Cowley would make up his mind to come bursting in, he said: 'What made you pick on the law?'

Ulrike smiled and moved her shoulders. She felt now she was in complete command, a martyr, a sacrifice; but the big gesture had been made. She could afford to gloat now . . .

'We start with the weakest link. British law is so wonderfully hypocritical. You kick an old woman to death, that's naughty. You get your wrist slapped.' She was working up her passionate feelings again. 'But do damage to some property – burn someone's Rolls Royce, break a few windows –'

The opening door and the arrival of a grim-faced George Cowley interrupted her. She glanced quickly, shrewdly, from Cowley's face to the message form in his hand. She seemed to hug herself, to grow, to bloom with the enormity of her glee.

Doyle took the note, read it, let his face betray deep and genuine concern.

'When was this?'

Cowley stood, blocky, his sandy hair glinting under the lights, looking like a hanging judge. 'Just after five.'

'Casualties?'

'Five dead . . . More than thirty injured . . .'

Gripping the message flimsy, Doyle swung around to confront Ulrike. He stared venomously at the girl terrorist.

'More of your handiwork.'

Ulrike was quite unconcerned about this policeman's passionate ill-feeling. He was upset, good!

'Really,' she said in a contemptuous off-hand manner.

'Which one was yours – Fleet Street, the Chambers in – ?'

She interrupted before he finished, flushed, boastful: 'Ryton Square. The Magistrate's Court.'

Ulrike's triumph blazed in the little room. In her mind's eye she could hear the eruption, see the flames and smoke, hear the stupid lawyers shrieking as they were blown up. She glowed with her victory for the cause in which she so passionately believed.

Doyle gave a single look at Cowley.

George Cowley picked up the phone, dialled the number standing like figures in his brain.

He spoke urgently.

'Cowley. It's Ryton Square SW3. A Magistrate's Court.'

He hung up.

Ulrike stared at Cowley, then at Doyle. She looked bewildered. Some of the triumph in her face wilted at the edges.

Doyle said: 'Can't win 'em all, love.'

'I don't,' said Ulrike, and her voice shook a little, carrying a suggestion, a merest hint, of panic. 'I don't understand.'

Doyle tapped his wrist watch.

'It isn't as late as you think. Your watch is fast.'

Instinctively, Ulrike lifted her wrist to look at the watch strapped there. Her brows drew down. She caught a little breath.

Watching her, Doyle saw she was still unsure.

'The flight announcements – ' she began, putting some of the old truculence back.

Doyle, smiling, interrupted.

'Ask 'em nicely, they'll say anything.'

How long does it take a savage beast of the jungle to realise he's fallen down a hole laid for him as a trap? How long to react, and leap upwards, snarling, wicked teeth clashing, vicious claws striking and scraping the sides of the pit?

Ulrike realised she had been duped.

She let out a shriek and rushed on Doyle. Her hands lifted into claws and she struck at him. She was panting and shrieking and striking out. She tried to bite him. She tried to kick him.

Doyle, an old-time copper used to handling people, even crazy female terrorists, evaded her attack and with Cowley's assistance managed to hold her still long enough for Polly Edwards and the assistants to take care of Ulrike.

The two CI5 men looked at the panting dishevelled figure. They could find it in their hearts to be sorry for her. Sorry as a misguided girl, paving her own personal road to hell with the best of intentions; but as a notorious terrorist captured and in the bag - no. No, for that kind of girl the CI5 men could only allow the Law which she held in so much contempt to deal with her.

Where Cowley and his people had been playing a waiting game, watching the hands of the clock tickaround, waiting to pounce, eternally waiting like everyone else in the airport, now they were catapulted into action. The location of the terrorists' car was discovered and the police cordoned off the area. The Bomb Squad were alerted to the exact situation and their team rolled in, equipped to handle the suspect car.

Cowley, Bodie and Doyle went by Cowley's Rover, driven with smooth speed through the traffic by Paula, rushed to the spot in Ryton Square where the action lay.

Although the square appeared seething with confusion, the police had their end of the operation under control.

People were being stopped from entering, all traffic was turned away by uniformed officers. Barriers were going up to keep back curious crowds, and these crowds were being dispersed as they formed by the time hallowed words, move along please.

The CI5 Rover was allowed through.

The members of the Bomb Squad team were already setting up their white ribbons to form a no-go area. Police were directing people pouring out of the Magistrate's Court, and others were making sure the adjoining buildings were empty. The busy bustle and activity met the CI5 men as they got out of the Rover.

The centre of interest stood beside the kerb.

In the window a large cardboard notice had been perched. It read: BROKEN DOWN.

The car was, like the others, nondescript. It might have just come off an auction lot, or been left unattended whilst its owner went for a quick cup of tea. The idea that this car, broken down and all, could be harbouring a device that could blow down the front of the building, smash windows and kill and maim many people, just would not occur to any law-abiding citizen walking past.

'Well, we found it,' said Doyle.

'Now it's up to the Bomb Squad,' said Bodie.

They could both think of occasions, hairy occasions, when they'd discovered bombs and had to go and defuse them themselves. It was nice and comforting to have the experts do it. Very.

The Bomb Squad handled everything by the book. They had their Pig parked far enough away to be safe. In the back of the van-like body of the Pig a sergeant manipulated the switches and controls of the Wheelbarrow. A monitor screen – black and white only so far – above the controls relayed what the electronic eyes of the Wheelbarrow picked up. The sergeant handled the remote-controlled Wheelbarrow very well, bringing it up to the suspect car, circling it, checking off the details. He made it fast; he also made it a thorough job.

Bodie and Doyle turned to where the bomb disposal expert finished settling his armour about him. He was a big chap, fresh-faced, bushy moustache. He wore the cumbersome bomb suit as though about to ride into a charge at Agincourt. The armour would protect him to a point; but no one had any illusions about what would happen if a bomb went off as he handled it. He started off, clumping towards the suspect car.

The three from CI5 watched, standing together, in another man's expertise and danger feeling their own close comradeship.

The only person now in danger from Ulrike's bomb was the bomb disposal expert. His helmeted head bent above the boot of the car. Cautiously he turned the handle and lifted. He moved very slowly and very gently. Inside he saw the bomb, the wires trailing in a more amateur fashion than he would have expected from the reputation of this little lot. The timing device tick-tocked away. He looked.

Watching him, Cowley, Bodie and Doyle saw the bomb disposal expert turn slowly and give the thumbs up sign. His squad, crouched ready to his rear, visibly relaxed.

The three CI5 men felt the tension evaporate.

It was all over.

They went off to the courthouse to settle some of the many details that would have to be finalised, Bodie and Doyle following Cowley.

The explosion was a big one.

The smash brought in its wake an enormous rolling thunder of echoes.

Black smoke coiled and leaped and twisted high over the Magistrates' Court.

The car had vanished. Hundreds of windows were tinkling into destruction. There was no sign through the masses of black smoke of the bomb disposal expert. Men were yelling. Sirens started up and klaxons blared.

Fire engines began to roar into the scene.

It was chaos.

Cowley, Bodie and Doyle just stood there. They saw the smoke and heard the noise, smelled the confusion and terror. This was the terrorists' idea of perfection. CI5 had done its job. They had found the last bomb before it exploded.

And, now, this . . .

They stared for half a dozen heartbeats at that appalling sight. Then they turned away, sickened. Their job was to attempt to combat the causes of this violence, to fight crime, and this they would continue to do.

One bomb however destructively terrifying would not stop the men of CI5, the Squad, the Big A . . .

JOE POYER

TUNNEL WAR

POLITICAL DYNAMITE!

In 1911 Europe was rushing headlong towards world war. And beneath the English Channel a massive tunnel was already under construction. When fire wreaked havoc in an unfinished tunnel shaft, James Bannerman, the project chief, smelt trouble. Further deadly 'accidents' confirmed his suspicions – the project was being systematically destroyed by a team of professional saboteurs.

Bannerman already faced an impossible choice: sacrifice the tunnel – or the lives of his men. But nothing had quite prepared him for the devastating web of murder and conspiracy that stretched from Ireland to Germany to the heart of Britain's political arena and which threatened to destroy everything he'd ever fought for – including his life . . .

WARLORDS

BY BOB LANGLEY

BRITAIN'S FUTURE?

Britain is on the verge of total collapse. North Sea oil has suddenly run dry. Rationing and unemployment spread like wildfire. And four elections in two months have plunged the nation into a terrifying chaos.

Across the Atlantic America decides it is time to step in and assist their one-time ally. BY FERMENTING NO LESS THAN A FULL-SCALE BLOODY REVOLUTION GUARANTEED TO BRING THE DYING NATION TO HER KNEES AND TO CHANGE THE COURSE OF WORLD HISTORY WITH ONE DEVASTATING, FINAL COUP DE GRÂCE . . .

Fast and furious, WARLORDS is a terrifying and disturbing vision of Britain at the mercy of the powerlords in the not-so-distant future!

ADVENTURE THRILLER 0 7221 5409 7 £1.25